LETTERS TO JUDY
WHAT KIDS WISH
THEY COULD TELL YOU

"My mom and dad aren't split up but they are always fighting. Sometimes I just want to yell out, 'Stop fighting!' But I can't . . ."

"I have a problem at school! One girl has decided to turn everyone against me. And on the bus another girl is doing the same thing . . ."

"My mother is going to law school. I don't know whether to be happy or sad. Sure, some of the mothers work, but no one as hard as my mother . . ."

"I don't have anyone to turn to. Once I got drunk and broke into a house and it was kind of fun. *No! I don't want to think that!*"

"Every single person I know is on something. It's impossible to sit around listening to people talk about being high constantly and not want to do it yourself . . ."

"I just broke up with my boyfriend. I still lose sleep over him. But my family doesn't understand. They say, 'Caroline, why lose sleep over him? He's not worth it.' How can I tell them that we made love off and on?"

A Literary Guild Alternate Selection

THE CRITICS PRAISE *LETTERS TO JUDY* . . .

P9-CSW-539

Praise for
LETTERS TO JUDY

"The children Blume introduces are such radiantly candid and innocent human beings that we cannot help but look at our own children with a deeper understanding and compassion . . . This is a generous book."

—*Washington Post Bookworld*

"This is a good jumping-off point for communication between parents and children . . . These messages cannot be given often enough."

—*ALA Booklist*

"Kids don't just trust Judy Blume, they pour their hearts out to her . . . *Letters to Judy* is a moving collective portrait of young Americans . . . The sound of real life practically leaps off the pages."

—*Los Angeles Herald Examiner*

"*Letters to Judy* is an unforgettable and painfully honest book . . . it should help a lot of young people for whom her works have literally been life savers."

—*Marlboro Enterprise*

"Judy Blume . . . lets children and adolescents know that although life can be painful, it need not be a solitary struggle . . . This book, like all her others, is one for parents and their children to share . . . a compassionate guide."

—*Psychology Today*

Praise for
JUDY BLUME

"Judy Blume has written 14 children's books, renowned for their compassion and honesty . . . She inspires the trust of children . . . Judy Blume tells it like it is."

—Houston Post

"Judy Blume has some special quality that speaks to a lot of lonely kids . . . She's unjudgmental, never lectures, is practical and understanding. Above all she seems to have total recall of the inmost feelings, woes and worries of the adolescent."

—The Star

"Ask almost any adolescent about novelist Judy Blume, and you'll hear that she's the only adult who knows—*really* knows—what it's like to be a kid."

—USA Today

"Judy Blume is Miss Lonelyhearts, Mister Rogers and Dr. Ruth rolled into one."

—The New York Daily News

"Judy Blume's books for children have won her a huge following . . . and children who identify with her characters trust Blume with their own secret fears and worries. It is a trust she takes seriously. Somehow, she always takes the time to listen—and makes the time to answer."

—Cleveland Plain Dealer

Books by Judy Blume

Forever . . .
Letters to Judy
Smart Women
Wifey

Published by POCKET BOOKS

Most Pocket Books are available at special quantity discounts for bulk purchases for sales promotions, premiums or fund raising. Special books or book excerpts can also be created to fit specific needs.

For details write the office of the Vice President of Special Markets, Pocket Books, 1230 Avenue of the Americas, New York, New York 10020.

Judy Blume

Letters To Judy

What Kids Wish They Could Tell You

PUBLISHED BY POCKET BOOKS NEW YORK

POCKET BOOKS, a division of Simon & Schuster, Inc.
1230 Avenue of the Americas, New York, N.Y. 10020

Copyright © 1986 by Kids Fund
Cover photograph copyright © 1986 Thomas Victor

Published by arrangement with G. P. Putnam's Sons
Library of Congress Catalog Card Number: 85-30119

All rights reserved, including the right to reproduce
this book or portions thereof in any form whatsoever.
For information address G. P. Putnam's Sons,
200 Madison Avenue, New York, N.Y. 10016

ISBN: 0-671-62696-5

First Pocket Books printing March 1987

10 9 8 7 6 5 4 3 2 1

POCKET and colophon are registered trademarks
of Simon & Schuster, Inc.

Printed in the U.S.A.

To my readers, who have shared their lives with me.

Thank you for your loyalty, your encouragement and your love. I hope you can feel mine coming back to you in this book.

Acknowledgments

I wish to express my thanks to my family, friends and colleagues for their patience during endless hours of discussion and for their support during the two years I have been working on this book. I would especially like to thank Beverly Horowitz, who helped me find the narrative thread, and Alan Pollack, M.D., and Charles De Stefano, Ph.D., for their time, their interest and their many helpful suggestions.

Judy Blume has arranged for all the royalties from the sale of this book to go directly to the Kids Fund, a nonprofit charitable and educational foundation.

The Kids Fund was established by Judy in response to the many letters she receives from her young readers saying they wish they could talk more openly and more honestly with their parents and have access to better sources of information about the matters that concern them.

Since 1981, the fund has provided more than $145,000 in grants to nonprofit organizations for support of programs that address these needs and concerns. This book is a further educational project of the Kids Fund, as well as a source of support for its continuing activities.

Contents

CONTENTS

CONTENTS

Introduction
HELP ME TELL MY PARENTS

I don't know any way to introduce this book except to tell you how and why it came about. In 1971 I received my first letter from a young reader. She was thirteen and she wrote to tell me that she was exactly like the character of Margaret in *Are You There God? It's Me, Margaret.* I was surprised and thrilled and I wrote back to her the same day. Somehow, between then and now, the number of kids who write to me has grown to nearly two thousand each month.

Why do kids confide in me? I've been trying to figure that out for years. I'm still not sure I understand completely, but I know that it's often easier to confide in someone you don't have to face at the breakfast table the next morning, someone who can't use anything you have to say against you. And I know from their letters they identify with the characters I've created in my books, so they feel that I'll also understand them, without judging or condemning them for their thoughts and feelings.

Dear Judy,

Whenever I have a fight with somebody I sit right down and write a letter to you. I don't always send it but it makes me feel better just to write it.

Jennifer, age 11

Writing to me is the kids' way of unloading what's on their minds. It's therapeutic. Writing can also be therapeutic for me. My brother tells me that every book I write saves me five years in therapy. I laugh about that but he could be right. Like most writers, when I began to write, I wrote out of my own needs. Writing was my way of dealing with and trying to make sense of life. It was my way of communicating. Writing for and about kids wasn't a conscious decision. I wrote what came naturally. I wrote about what was important to me. I wrote the kinds of books I wanted to read when I was young, books about real life and real feelings.

Dear Judy,

I think the main point of kids' books is to show that things that happen to you also happen to other kids. It makes kids feel like they are normal. I thought I was weird for doing and thinking some things but your books make me feel okay.

Brian, age 13

Dear Judy,

My mom never talks about the things young girls think most about. She doesn't know how I feel. I don't know where I stand in the world. I don't know who I am. That's why I read. To find myself.

Elizabeth, age 13

Dear Judy,
    Everyone thinks I'm so sweet but I have some feelings that no one knows about.

Laurie, age 12

For a long time I've thought about sharing these letters with other kids, to show them that they're not the only ones, that they're not as alone as they think. But I wasn't sure how to do it, so I kept putting it off. And then I heard from Amy:

Dear Judy,
    Please write a book for *adults* about our problems to open their eyes.

Amy, age 10

It was this letter from Amy that opened *my* eyes. She reminded me that what most of the kids are really saying is: "Please, Judy . . . help me tell my parents. I want to talk to them about personal subjects but I don't know how. I wish I could ask them questions but I'm too afraid. Nobody ever talks about what's really on my mind, either at home or at school."

In 1983 I began to sift through the cartons of special letters I had saved over the years, wondering if I could find a way to share them without betraying the kids' confidence, not only with other kids, but with the adult world as well.

During the next two-and-a-half years, whenever friends or colleagues asked what I was working on I would tell them about this project. They would listen intently, nod, and say, "Oh, letters from deeply troubled kids." Then I would try to explain that yes, some of the letters are from troubled kids, but most are from kids who love their parents and get along in school, although they still sometimes feel alone, afraid and misunderstood. Kids like yours and mine. Kids who are convinced that if only I would write a book about their experiences, their problems, their feelings, those closest to them would finally understand.

If you're wondering why your child would write to me instead of coming to you, let me assure you that you're not alone. There were times when my daughter, Randy, and son, Larry, didn't come to me either. And that hurt. Like every parent, I've made a million mistakes raising my kids, as you'll see when you read this book. And I certainly don't have all the answers. It's just a lot easier to sound wise when you're talking about someone else's family.

If I had had access to these letters when Randy and Larry were young I think it would have helped. I can't say it would have prevented every problem or every mistake. No book can do that. But these letters might have made me more aware of my children's feelings. And awareness goes a long way.

I write fiction. I'm not a psychiatrist, psychologist or family therapist, and it's certainly never been my intention to give advice. But I can't ignore the pleas of the kids who write to me. When I answer the kinds of letters you will find in this book, I don't attempt to give specific advice. I try to be supportive. I encourage them to talk to their parents first. I may suggest that they write their parents a letter, like the letter they wrote to me, if they feel they can't approach them in any other way. I tell them that if their parents aren't listening to confide in someone else, someone they can trust. Above all, I tell them not to worry alone. And there are times, when it seems that they really can't handle the situation, that I urge them to ask for professional help.

Sometimes I become more emotionally involved in their lives than I should. There are letters that tear me apart, and they will you, too, the anguish is so great. There have been times when I've consulted with family therapists and psychiatrists to help me help kids because I didn't know what else to do. When I can refer a young reader or a family to an agency or materials that might help I feel better. (A list of such resources appears in the back of the book.)

The letters in this book offer an intimate look at kids today—kids speaking in their own voices about their worries, their concerns and their relationships with friends and family. Names, places and other identifying facts have been changed as needed to protect the privacy of the children and their families. Occasionally, grammar and spelling have been corrected, in order not to detract from substance. If, as you're reading these letters, you think that you recognize yourself or your family, remember that almost every one of them could have been written by a hundred different kids. They all are excerpts and a few are composites.

Of course there are other things on kids' minds besides what they are writing about to me. I have had very few letters about childhood fears. I have never had a letter from a young person with anorexia or any other eating disorder. I have never had a letter from a child about nuclear war, yet I know a twelve-year-old boy who cannot sleep at night because he is so afraid. Kids write to me about their most immediate concerns, often prompted by the experiences of the characters in my books.

During the years I was working on this project, immersed in the kids' letters, my own thoughts and feelings surfaced. I remembered events that I hadn't thought about in years. When it came time to tie the book together I wanted to share with the kids what they had shared with me—moments from my own life, both as a child and as a parent. I hope that these letters and anecdotes will help you remember what it was like to be young and help your kids feel less alone.

Chapter I
I LOVE MY PARENTS, BUT . . .

1

They Don't Understand Me

Dear Judy,

This isn't a crash catastrophe emergency letter or anything. I just need to talk to you. My mother is terrific and is the closest one to me. But I need someone else. Someone who, if I talk about my feelings and opinions, will understand me. Someone who will really *listen*.

Diana, age 12

When I was growing up I didn't doubt my parents' love for me, but I didn't think they understood me, or had any idea of what I was really like. And I made no effort to try to change that. I just assumed that parents don't understand their kids, ever. That there is a lot of pretending in family life.

As a parent I've experienced the other side of the coin. During a particularly rough time for our family, my daughter, Randy, confessed to someone else that she wasn't telling me the truth about how she was feeling because she sensed that I only wanted to hear that everything was wonderful. Well, everything wasn't wonderful and Randy found a way to let me know—by acting out her feelings. Kids often act out instead of telling what's on their minds. We need to listen to each other more carefully, even when we aren't speaking in words.

Dear Judy,

What I wrote for is that I've got a problem. I just turned twelve and since then my mother and I haven't been so close. I don't see her all day. Then, when she comes home from work, she's so tired and ill I don't get to talk to her much.

We've always been so close and now this. I'm really scared and I don't know how to tell her or how to let my feelings out in the open. I hope you don't mind me asking you but I had no one else to turn to. My father wouldn't understand and I'd be embarrassed to say anything to him. Have you ever slowly been separated from someone you love?

Samantha, age 12

Dear Judy,

I often daydream in school but I always get my work in on time. My mother is tough and sometimes I feel so mad I want to run away from her and everyone else. My dad is soft. He does everything she says. I like my dad better but I would not say that to my mother.

Cathy, age 11

Dear Judy,

I wish the relationship between me and my father could be better. I feel guilty that when he was transferred to South America for a year I only missed him very little. Is that natural? Then, when he came back, we moved. The first year I was here I used to cry and nobody found out. Then, this year, I've been yelling and screaming at everybody and getting into trouble. Please, can you help me?

Judith, age 13

Dear Judy,

I am twelve years old. I have a brother who is a month old and parents who take advantage of me. The main reason I am writing is I want your advice. Ever since my mom had the baby I don't have any privacy. They expect me to do everything (clean the house, take care of the cats, etc.) but since I just started seventh grade I have a lot of tests and homework. They expect me to get my homework done in an hour so I can do my chores. Well, it's impossible.

I've tried explaining my side but they don't understand. I've told my friends and they don't know what I should do. Do you know what I should do? Please, I need your help. Another thing I meant to tell you was my parents also make fun of me. They say I have a bad personality or I'm getting chunky and other things that really hurt. I really would like your advice. Thanks!

Kimberly, age 12

Dear Judy,

Nothing I do is good enough for my father. If I get all A's and one B he says I could have had all A's if only I had tried harder. If I am elected co-captain of the soccer team he asks why I wasn't elected captain. He expects me to be perfect. I lie sometimes to get him off my back.

Josh, age 13

It's hard for kids to admit that they are less than perfect when *perfect* is what they think we want them to be—or expect them to be. Many of our kids don't confide in us because they don't want us to be hurt or disappointed. They feel inadequate if they can't meet our expectations so they pretend in order to please us and then feel guilty because they know the truth. When I was young I did that.

My brother, to this day, cannot hear the name Richie Robinson without cringing. Richie Robinson lived down the street from us, and throughout my brother's school years he heard, "If only you were more like Richie Robinson." Richie Robinson represented perfection to our mother. He was the perfect son, the perfect student, the perfect citizen. And most of all Richie Robinson never gave his parents any trouble, at least none that we knew about. I'm sure my brother had fantasies of Richie Robinson's downfall. I know I did. I saw the headlines in my mind: RICHIE ROBINSON FAILS TENTH GRADE; RICHIE ROBINSON PLAYS WRONG NOTES AT PIANO RECITAL; RICHIE ROBINSON ARRESTED FOR STEALING TOMATO PLANTS FROM NEIGHBOR.

It's hard on kids, too, when they think we don't appreciate them and can't accept them the way they are. A young teenager, Meredith, once told me that her mother would never accept her because she wasn't tall and thin and blonde. (Her mother was.) Meredith's mother denied this, explaining that Meredith didn't understand. My mother often tells me that I didn't understand what was really going on in our family when I was young. But my perception of my early years is what matters to me, just as Meredith's perception of her mother's feelings about her looks is what counts. We have subtle ways of letting our kids know how we feel about them. And our kids are certainly affected by those feelings.

Dear Judy,

I would really like to help you with your writing career so I've thought up some ideas for books and some of them are about family.

My first topic is about a mother committing suicide. You also could have in it something about coping without a mother.

My second topic is about a mother being kidnapped, then raped and tied with a rope and then thrown off a bridge. She is still alive and makes it to shore okay. She then walks about a mile and catches a ride. She tells the driver to drop her off at the hospital and the driver does. The woman goes into the hospital and tells the nurse her whole story. All this time the woman's child is at home, alone, and knows nothing about the whole thing.

My third topic is about a mother who writes bad checks and her husband tells her not to write another one or else he won't want to see her again. The mother writes checks to buy things that she won't ever use. The man and woman have three boys and one little girl. The little girl is probably going to be sent to live with her grandparents.

Lynn, age 11

When kids are angry or disappointed in us and don't know how to say so, they might think up bad things that could happen. They don't necessarily understand that thinking about it can't really make it happen, and afterward they blame themselves for whatever goes wrong.

When I was young I scared myself by imagining terrible things that could happen to my family. I suppose I had some of those fantasies because I was afraid to show my anger. I felt that my mother often blamed me for things I couldn't control, like the day my friend gagged on an ice cube and threw up on our porch, or the day another friend accidentally spilled a bottle of flesh-colored acne medicine on my dark blue bedroom rug. I understand now that my mother wasn't really angry at me, but angry that those accidents happened in the first place and that someone, probably her, would have to clean up the mess. Yet what I remember is how I felt at the time.

When Randy was growing up and angry with me, she would write me letters about how she was feeling and slip them under my bedroom door. She let out some of her anger through her writing. And I learned a lot about her feelings from reading those letters.

Larry had no trouble showing his anger. He would shout and kick and get it all out and once he did, he was ready to be my friend again. He still says what's on his mind but he doesn't have temper tantrums anymore.

My mother used to say, "We never have to punish Judy . . . if you look at her wrong, she cries." Well, yes . . . but I wish I had been able to risk showing my anger now and then. I wish I had felt secure enough to know that once I had gotten it all out I would still be loved.

2

My Brother and Sister Get All the Attention

Dear Judy,

I have a problem that I cannot tell my mom about or she'll get mad. My sister is two years younger than me and she gets all the attention. For example, when I don't let her play with one of my Barbies she goes and tells. Of course she gets to play with everything of mine, but if I want to play with something of hers, Mom will say, "Give that back to Gena!" It doesn't seem fair.

Rebecca, age 9

I often write about sibling rivalry because it is such an important part of family life. My aunt used to tell me stories about being the youngest in a family of three. My mother was the oldest, my uncle was three years younger, and Frances, my aunt, was three years younger than he was. Frances said that my mother was pampered and got everything she wanted because she was the first child and my grandparents were ecstatically happy to have her. She said that my mother was given milk baths so that she'd have beautiful skin, her hair was curled each night and she had the best clothes.

My uncle got a lot of attention, too, because he was the only son. Frances said that by the time she was born no one was very interested in her. (That's how she saw it, anyway.) My mother and uncle were taken on exciting trips, but Frances, the baby, was always left at home. She felt less important than her older brother and sister.

Dear Judy,

My mother is very mean to me. You see, I have this brother, Darren. He is Mom's little angel. In cars, if I turn around to look out the back window, she says, "Stop making faces at Darren, Roxanne!" But every time I turned around *he* was making faces at me. I told this to my mother. She just shrugged. She always blames me, never Darren.

Darren has done plenty of mean things himself. He once, when I took him to the park, pushed me off the bars. I had to run home crying in front of all my friends. I got this big bump on my forehead and was dizzy the rest of the day. And my mom didn't even punish him! What should I do to make my mother understand?

Roxanne, age 9

Dear Judy,

I am in fifth grade and I have to tell you something. It's about me and my brother. He is always picking on me and whenever he doesn't get his way he cries and he punches me. My sister is a problem too. She always makes fusses and tells me what to do.

Eileen, age 10

Dear Judy,
   My older brother is always teasing me and beating me up. Whenever my parents go out he beats me up. What should I do?

Warren, age 9

My brother, David, is four years older than I am. He didn't beat me up, but he did tease me. When he had friends over he would say to them, "Watch this!" And then he would trick me in some way and I would wind up sprawled across the floor. David and his friends would laugh. In some ways I liked this teasing and attention from my older brother and his friends. But when I became a teenager I didn't want them to see me as a clown, as part of a Punch-and-Judy team. I wanted them to see me as a young woman.
   David was five years ahead of me in school. We really didn't relate that much as we were growing up. He was basically a loner, preferring to spend his time in the basement workshop, building intricate models or working on his inventions, rather than out on the street with friends. He left for college as I was beginning eighth grade, and after that I was the only child at home. I don't remember feeling jealous or envious or competitive with my brother. "Why should you have?" he

asked me recently, when we were discussing our early years. "You got all the attention. You were everybody's little darling." I was surprised to hear him say that although it is probably true.

Yet I knew, from overhearing adult conversations, that David was supposed to be a genius. That was the reason he had started school a year early. That was why he could build his own radio and oscilloscope and make fabulous creatures out of construction paper or eggshells. He never did very well at school though. He never felt that he fit in with the other kids, either.

Perhaps because I saw (or thought I saw) my parents' disappointment in him, since he did not fulfill their expectations, I believed that I had to please them in the ways that David did not. No one ever said that I was a genius, but I always got good grades and was socially active. Life for me has always been easier than for my brother. Maybe because he was the first child and I was the second. Maybe our parents were just more relaxed the second time around. Or maybe there is no way to explain it at all.

Dear Judy,

I have this problem and maybe you could write a book about it. I am in sixth grade and am eleven years old. But I look like a third grader that's just eight or nine years old. I have a sister whose name is Stephanie. She is in fifth grade and is a year younger than me. She is much taller than me and looks much older. When we are together people say that Stephanie should be in sixth grade and I should be in third or fourth. One person might try and guess how old I was and would say eight or nine. This is what makes me mad, or insults me. I think probably other people have had this problem but I'm not sure.

Erika, age 11

Dear Judy,

I have a problem that I hope you can answer. My problem is: I just can't seem to do anything right. I don't have much going for me. I can't write a poem, or draw, or even sing right. The reason I say that is because my sister can do all of that. She is very creative. She's got a lot going for her, besides her school grades. She just left the school that I'm now in. All the teachers there thought I would be just like her! They were wrong. I wasn't like her and so they were disappointed, I could tell. They treated me different before they found out that I wasn't great like my sister.

Tanya, age 12

Dear Judy,

I have an idea for one of your next books. It could be about a ten-year-old girl with a smaller sister, age nine. It wouldn't sound like much if it was just that, but it would sound better if the nine-year-old was mentally retarded. The bigger sister has problems with the younger one. She always breaks toys, throws big fits over little things and wants to cut the grass with a pair of scissors. She doesn't understand that her bigger sister is getting a little older and does not want to do the things she used to like to do, like playing house with pretend monkeys (instead of pretend babies). The little sister is scared of owls and loud noises. Please write a story about them for me.

Patricia, age 10

Dear Judy,

I know that there are other children who write you and have worse problems than I do, but I just have to get this out and tell somebody.

Here it is: it seems that my parents pay more attention to my sister because this is her last year living with us. You see, she is a big, bad twelfth grader and after she graduates she wants to go to college. Well, I don't think it's fair just because it's her last year at home and I don't know how to handle it because I'm used to my mother talking to me all the time. But not anymore. Now she is always talking to my sister, Valerie.

Do you know that for Christmas I got my mother a glass horse, because she collects glass animals, and when she opened it she seemed really happy and excited. She said, "Oh, Cheryl . . . it's beautiful! I love it! Thank you very much." Now, there's nothing wrong with what she said but when she started to open my sister's present my father ran into his room, got his camera, came back and took a picture of my mother opening the present from Valerie. And do you know what? Valerie got her a glass cat and her cat was much smaller than my horse but my mother seemed more excited by Valerie's present.

Well, I'll just have to face this problem the way it is. Anyway, Valerie will be gone after she graduates and then things will be back to normal again. At least I hope so.

Cheryl, age 11

My own two children were very different. Randy, who is two years older, was shy, quiet, sweet and anxious to please. She was sensitive and artistic and would read for hours, or paint or work on her stamp collection. Larry, the family entertainer, was outgoing, inquisitive, and imaginative. He was openly affectionate, yet he was fearful and saw monsters in his room at night. Like all siblings, they competed for our attention and approval.

They were very close during their early years, fought their ways through the middle years of childhood and were not sympathetic to each other's adolescent rebellions. They became good friends again when they were older teenagers.

I hope they will stay close. After all, they have shared the ups and downs of family life. I hope someday, if they choose to have children, their children will be close. But this is just a mother's dream.

My brother and I weren't close for years. We barely talked. We were strangers, living in different worlds. Now, in our forties, we have come back together. We are friends. We can sit for hours reminiscing about our early years, about our family life. If my mother is present she will sometimes shake her head and say, "It wasn't anything like that." But for us, it was.

Family relationships are so intense and so complicated that some of us spend a lifetime trying to figure them out. As children (even grown up ones) we tend to blame our parents for our problems. As parents we feel responsible for our children's problems. In Lynn

Caine's book, *What Did I Do Wrong? Mothers, Children, Guilt,* she discusses the way mothers automatically feel guilty for everything that goes wrong with their kids. I understand, intellectually, that I am not solely responsible for every problem my children have, but emotionally—well, that's another story. I am still full of if onlys . . . *if only I had done that differently, if only I had listened more carefully.*

I tell Randy, who also writes, that if she invents mothers who behave horribly in her stories I'll try not to take it personally. But I know that my mother doesn't react well to books of mine that have less than wise and loving mothers, even when I assure her that the characters I invent don't necessarily have anything to do with my own life.

There is no such thing as perfection in family life, as much as we might wish for it. We do the best we can and hope it will all work out.

3

I Am Adopted And . . .

Dear Judy,

I am thirteen and in the eighth grade. I need help with a problem that I have. My mother is always telling me what to do, when she doesn't even do it herself. She is not my real mother. I am adopted. But when I say anything about trying to find my real mother, she has a fit. I hope you can help me.

Jessie, age 13

A twelve-year-old friend of mine, who was adopted as an infant, once told me, "I can make my mother cry anytime I want to. All I have to say is, 'You're not my real mother!'" At the time I thought that was the most cruel remark I had ever heard from a child. And I wondered why she would say such a thing.

But I have learned, through reading and research, that adolescents who have been adopted often face a more complicated set of problems than other young people, and that for them, breaking away can be especially painful. Curiosity about birth parents is normal for adopted children and shouldn't be seen as a threat to the parents who have lovingly raised them. Nor should it be used as a weapon by the adopted child.

Even young kids who are not adopted sometimes have fantasies about being adopted. They feel that they don't belong in their families so they must have come from somewhere else. Otherwise they would fit in, they would be more like their parents and their siblings, and certainly, their families would understand them. A six-year-old, who had just been scolded by his mother, told me that his *real* mother was a princess. That the hospital had made a mistake and switched him with another baby when he was born. If only he could find this princess, who was beautiful, kind and very rich, he knew that she would appreciate him and never blame him for something he did not do. And she would let him buy as many bags of Reese's Pieces as he wanted.

Dear Judy,

I am only eleven and my mom is trying to make me into something I am not. I have a real close friend, Colleen, and we get along just great. She has had some terrible experiences in the past and I told my mom about them. I am really mad with myself and my mother because for one, I told her something I shouldn't of said about my friend's past, and now my mom won't even let me go over to her house.

She has hurt me in more ways, such as she is always yelling at me to join the kind of people I don't fit into. I have had some rough times in my life, especially when I found out I had been adopted at two months. It has been so bad with me and my family I have even thought of running away.

But there is one thing that really makes me mad. And that is if my mom has had a bad day at work she'll take it all out on me and then the next day she will be really nice and take me somewhere. The third day she'll be a witch again.

I never tell her anything or ask for advice because she'll start picking on me. But Colleen is a true friend and I can confide in her and she can confide in me. My mom may be nice sometimes but it will never change the way I feel about her and my family. I am glad there is you that people can confide in.

P.S. Should I see a psychologist?

Annie, age 11

Kids: There is no way that I can say if Annie needs to see a psychologist or not. Some problems persist and grow and make it hard to get on with your life. At those times it's a good idea to ask for help. If you can't ask your parents, you should ask someone at school to help you find a professional.

Dear Judy,

It has been my dream for quite some time to write a book geared to teenagers who have been adopted. I have been through this experience myself and am now an adult adoptee associated with an adult search group as a search assistant.

So many of us went through a very strange adjustment period in our teens compounded by the feeling that we were rejected, not fully under-standing the different situations that could lead a mother to surrender her child. The teenaged adoptee feels that he or she is the only one who has had these feelings. They need to realize that every adoptee has special doubts and problems.

I must admit that I really don't know why I am writing. Possibly to use you as a sounding board, maybe even for encouragement. I need to find the words to let these kids know that the mystery behind their adoptions is not their fault. That just because adoptive parents won't talk about it, the circumstances surrounding their births weren't something terrible, as I have found most teenaged adoptees believe. They can't understand why their adoptive parents feel threatened because they are curious to know who their birth mothers were and why they were given away.

I have the need to let adopted kids know these things so they won't have the self-doubts that I had all those terrible years. They need to know that they are not alone in the way that they have been feeling.

Debra, adult

4

I Wish They Were Like Everyone Else

Dear Judy,

I wrote to you because I have a lot of problems and I really want to talk to someone but I didn't know who. I finally decided on you. I will keep writing to you and telling you things. I will tell you one problem per letter.

I guess I'll start with my family. I am growing up and I care more and more about what people look like and things like that. I have a brother, Scott, who is in sixth grade. He is very out of style and very dependent on other people. He plays the piano. He's been playing it for nine years. I am very jealous. My brother is not popular and he is pretty ugly, too. Also, he is not very responsible. My parents spend a lot of time with him.

My mom is out of style and whenever a friend comes over she makes a fool of herself. She tells bad jokes and worst of all, I can't talk to her about anything such as boyfriends. I don't know what to do about her. I'll tell you more about me and my family in my next letter. And please respond. I really need some advice and listening.

Beth, age 10

Dear Judy,

My name is Ramona and I'm ten. I live in Seattle and I have one younger brother and a thirteen-year-old sister who's a brat.

My mother is going to law school. I don't know whether to be happy or sad. All my friends' mothers are housewives. Sure, some of the mothers work but no one as hard as my mother. She leaves at 7:15 A.M. and doesn't get home until 9 or 10 P.M. She wears old blue jeans just about every day. Everyone else's mother always wears skirts.

Ramona, age 10

A friend of mine, Barbara Girion, wrote a book called *Like Everybody Else* about a girl whose mother is a writer and a bit eccentric. In the story, she wishes her mother could be like everyone else's mother. I guess all kids experience those feelings at one time or another. They don't want us to embarrass them. They don't want us to stand out in a crowd or draw attention to ourselves. Although all of my friends adored my father I can still remember saying, "Oh, Daddy . . . please!" when I felt he was behaving in an embarrassing way.

A few years ago, when Randy was in college, George, the man in my life, and I went to visit her with George's daughter, Amanda, who was then about fifteen. As we waited on line at a restaurant, George and I were clowning around and Amanda, embarrassed by our behavior, kept inching farther and farther away from us. Randy finally took her aside and said, "Look . . . they may seem eccentric to you now, but when you're my age you'll appreciate them."

Well, I couldn't believe it! Just a few years before there was nothing I could do right as far as Randy was concerned. Both of my kids went through a period of becoming so hypercritical and rejecting that it was a relief when they finally went off to college.

My friend, Marian, a happily married, successful lawyer and a devoted mother, has a sixteen-year-old daughter, Lesley, who is beginning to break away. Marian and Lesley have always been close and they are very much alike. Now Lesley is critical of everything her mother says and does, from her looks, to her work, to her politics. Lesley is quick to let Marian know she considers her a failure, as a parent and as a person. Marian finds Lesley's behavior unbearably painful. She is trying hard to win back Lesley's approval, and the harder she tries the swifter Lesley is to reject her. Lesley will be applying to college in the fall and the following year she will be leaving home, so she is getting ready by proving to herself that she can make it on her own, without her mother.

I encouraged Marian to get some counseling to help her through this rough time. Nobody can stand being treated as the enemy in her own home for very long. I shared some of my experiences with her, too, especially my delight in finding that four years later both Randy and Larry emerged from college almost as sweet and loving as they once were. The anger and hostility had disappeared, replaced by the desire to understand their families and themselves. No one had prepared me for this part of parenthood. Everyone talks about adolescent rebellion but no one discusses the rewards of having lived through it. Now, as I watch them facing the real world—life after school—I wish I could reach out and protect them, saving them from all the inevitable mistakes. But I know I can't. I ask myself how well I have prepared them for this time of life. And the answer is, I don't know, but I feel optimistic.

Chapter II
LIFE AT SCHOOL AND LIFE WITH FRIENDS

1

It's Not Always the Greatest

Dear Judy,
  I'm having a bad time. Everything at school is going wrong.

Tricia, age 10

In our family my brother is famous for having kicked his kindergarten teacher in the stomach. He never did learn to like school. Years later, when Larry was in kindergarten, he would roll around on the floor in the morning, clutching his stomach, hoping that he wouldn't have to face another day in the classroom. Having seen the results of being turned off by school at an early age through my brother, I was determined to find the cause of Larry's unhappiness. It took weeks to discover that, as Larry puts it now, he was failing cutting. It turned out that Larry was the only left-handed child in his kindergarten class and the blunt-edged scissors were designed for right-handed children.

My aunt, an elementary school principal, saved the day by bringing Larry a pair of left-handed scissors. Today we can laugh about that incident, but it was very serious at the time.

It's hard for me to write this section because I come from a family of teachers. I once asked my mother, "If you could live your life over again would you do anything differently?" "Yes," she answered, "I would be a teacher." She raised me to be a teacher. I graduated from the School of Education at New York University, where I majored in early childhood education. But I never actually taught. I don't know if I would have been a good teacher or not. I don't know if I would have had the necessary patience and understanding.

Until I wrote the book *Blubber* I created classroom teachers who were, for the most part, kind and sensitive, which reflected my admiration for my aunt and uncle. I know how many dedicated classroom teachers there are. I hear from them every year. And when I was growing up I was lucky enough to have some of them myself. These teachers treat their students with respect. They understand that everything that happens outside the classroom affects their students' performance and behavior within. They are sure enough of themselves and their abilities to talk calmly and openly with the kids and with their parents. They are able to welcome differences of opinion. But not all kids are lucky enough to be blessed with such teachers every year. That is reality. And that is what the letters in this section are about.

Dear Judy,

My son's first-grade teacher is especially cruel to the boys in her class. She pulls their hair, raps them on their heads with her ballpoint pen and humiliates them in front of the other children. My son says if he was not a good reader it would be even worse for him. The boys who have trouble reading get the brunt of their teacher's rage.

I have tried talking to the principal but he did not want to hear what I had to say and he never allows children to change classes. I have tried talking to the other parents in the neighborhood but they are apathetic. I cannot afford private school tuition and I don't know what else to do. I feel powerless.

Elaine, adult

And that is exactly how most kids feel—powerless—especially when it comes to their lives in school. Going to school is a child's work. It is usually their first experience interacting with the world on their own.

Dear Judy,

My fourth-grade teacher cares more about how our classroom looks to visitors than about us. Take me, I am very short but I have to sit at a desk that is way too big for me. I asked my teacher to please get me a smaller desk but she said that would make the rows uneven. I told my mother but she says teachers can make the rows any way they want to. What can I do to get somebody to understand?

Lisa, age 9

Dear Judy,

I am in sixth grade. My teacher says I am a complete airhead. She gives me sickeningly low marks. I feel that I have the potential and desire to really be something, maybe an author or a journalist. But my teacher says I wouldn't be dedicated to my work enough. I try my best to show her she is wrong, but nothing works. She will never like me or think that my work is any good. I hate how she calls on me when I don't raise my hand. But when I do, she acts like she doesn't see it.

Christine, age 11

Dear Judy,

My teacher is always doing her nails and cutting out coupons. If one person talks when we are supposed to be quiet, she yells at us and keeps us after school. She makes us write one hundred times, *I will not talk out of turn.* So this one time I got really mad and instead of writing that, I wrote her a letter about how it isn't fair to punish all of us every time. But you know what? She never read my letter. I know because I watched her through the window in our classroom door and she dumped all our papers in the trash can as soon as we were gone.

Miriam, age 10

My daughter, Randy, had a teacher like Miriam's. She would come home from school angry almost every day. I approached the school principal but he told me

Randy's teacher had years of experience, and he wasn't going to interfere with her methods. There was no way I could solve Randy's problem. All I could do was empathize and encourage her to talk about her feelings. I think it helped just to let her know I was on her side.

2

What If It Happens to Me?

Dear Judy,
    I have a problem at school! One girl has decided to turn everyone against me. And on the bus another girl is doing the same thing. So now all the kids and even some of the teachers hate me! Have you written any books in which the main character has the same problem? If so, which one? If not, could you please write one?

Felicia, age 10

When Randy was a fifth grader, she came home from school with stories about her classmates and how badly they were treating each other. Randy was a shy, quiet child, not a member of the "In Group." She was an observer. And she was especially upset by the way one girl in her class, Cindy, had become the victim of the class leader. One day during lunch period, the leader of the class and her group locked Cindy in a supply closet and held a mock trial. Cindy was found guilty. "Guilty of what?" I asked Randy at the dinner table. But Randy didn't know. Guilty of lack of power is my guess.

What happened to Cindy could have happened to almost anyone. Randy knew that and it was a frightening thought. I asked Randy if the teacher knew what was going on. Randy didn't think so. Most of the harassment took place during lunch period or on the playground or on the school bus.

That episode led me to write the book *Blubber*, which deals with children's cruelty to each other.

Dear Judy,

Some of your books almost tell my life, like *Iggie's House*. I moved into a white neighborhood like that and I am black. And now *Blubber*. You see, my friends on the school bus aren't really my friends. They just step on me like I am a piece of dirt. When I get on the bus and try to sit down they say, "Oh, this seat is taken." So I ask, "Whose is it?" So they say, "Oh, it's Molly's or Jane's," or something like that. So then I go over to Molly or Jane who are sitting someplace else and I ask, "Is that your seat over there?" And they say, "Yes, that's my seat and you can't sit in it." And then they laugh. So I go up front and sit with the boys. The boys never act that way to me.

I am too soft to do anything to the girls because I always say to myself, Oh, let them have their fun. And then I always wind up getting my feelings hurt. I believe in God so much that I won't hit them. It says in the Bible to forgive your enemies and I try. But really (and nobody knows this) I am a very violent person. I try to hold it back and keep cool, so no one will ever guess the truth. But now I think I have to do something, something to show them I am not a piece of dirt.

Please write back and tell me what to do before I get violent and hurt someone.

Emma, age 11

Dear Judy,

If I was going to write a book I would write a book about a boy named Teddy. He would be a kid in fifth grade that everyone hated. He would have all kinds of problems with other people and then one day he thinks, I don't like being teased so I'm going to do something about it! So he does. But I don't know what.

Teddy, age 10

Dear Judy,

During sixth grade I was talked about, spread rumors about and embarrassed. I have tried everything sensible. I have ignored them and I have laughed with them. Nothing works and I am about to go crazy.

Vicki, age 12

Dear Judy,

I am a thirteen-year-old boy. When I was in sixth grade everyone liked me. No one ever teased me. In fact, kids I didn't even know stopped in the halls and said, "Hi, Billy!"

Everything changed in seventh grade. The school was a big difference. It was a junior/senior high. Our area has no middle school and kids go from sixth grade (in elementary school) to seventh grade in a school with seniors! This was the whole problem. In gym class all the tenth, eleventh, and twelfth graders would pick on me and say things like, "Here comes the school fag," or even more blunt things.

I told the principal and he said there was nothing he or anyone else could do about it. He said I just had to take it like all the other kids.

They did it the whole time I was in school. I was tripped, kicked and spit on to mention a few. One day it was too much. My whole lunch—Salisbury steak, mashed potatoes and milk, went over one kid's head. The other one got nicely pushed in a garbage can.

During all the time I was teased I escaped with reading. That's when I discovered your books. I could really relate with the teasing in *Blubber* although I'm not fat. All I can say is, thank you for being there when you were needed most.

Billy, age 13

When I read these letters I try to imagine having a job where my co-workers harass me or threaten me physically. A job where my boss is so out of touch that he or she has no idea what's going on. I imagine I feel anxious, fearful and desperate but I still have to get up every morning and drag myself to that place of work. When I get there, I can't concentrate. Eventually I throw up my hands and shout, "I quit!" Then I look for a new job.

But kids don't have that option, which is one reason I get so angry when I hear parents say, "You think you have problems now! Just wait. You don't even know what problems are." But they do know. And their problems can be as important as ours.

A librarian, Charlotte, wrote that when she was in fifth grade she was teased and tormented by her classmates. Her parents knew nothing about it. She was ashamed to tell them what was happening. This experience so colored Charlotte's attitude toward herself that to this day—and she is thirty-five—she does not expect people to like her.

During the middle years of childhood, from nine to thirteen, some kids use friendship to manipulate others. They use friendship to gain power. Larry was a sunny, friendly, outgoing child. We moved when he was in fifth grade and he started a new school, where most of the children had been together for many years. The leader of that class was Jeffrey, a physically small boy, but a powerful presence in the classroom. For months Larry suffered under his reign. I didn't know exactly what was going on but I knew there was trouble. At night Larry couldn't fall asleep. Sometimes he became physically ill. He wasn't able to verbalize his problem. Kids are sometimes ashamed to admit that they are victims in the classroom. Years later Larry told me that Jeffrey had threatened to kill him and Larry had believed that he would. That's enough to give anyone stomach pains.

Dear Judy,

My name is Melanie. I had a problem similar to the one you wrote about in *Blubber*. I was tormented and harassed at school. For two weeks

I was a wreck. The fear was sickening! Finally, I couldn't stand it anymore and I told my mom. We went to the principal. He straightened everything out. I just want to emphasize that when someone is harassed they should first try to handle it by themselves. If that doesn't work then they should head for the authorities.

Melanie, age 11

Every class has a leader but not every leader uses power in an evil way. A lot depends on the teacher. A teacher can't prevent every act of cruelty within the classroom, but he or she can go a long way in reducing it by being sensitive to the students, providing an atmosphere that is warm, secure and free from fear, and bringing the subject of how we treat each other out in the open. With that kind of teacher Larry's first few months in a new school might have been different.

What surprises me is how willing some kids are to reverse roles. The one who has been victimized will often, if given the chance, jump right in and participate in the victimization of someone else.

So if your kids come home from school with stories about their classmates and how they are treating each other, talk with them about it. Encourage them to get their fears and feelings out in the open. It's important for kids to sense their parents' real commitment to the idea that they become compassionate people.

As Jill's mother reminds her in *Blubber:* "Think how you would feel if it happened to you. Try to put yourself in her place."

"I could never be in her place," Jill replies.

"Don't be so sure," her mother says.

45

Kids: If it happens to you try to solve it yourself, as Melanie advises. But if you can't, you have to find someone you can trust—a parent, a teacher, a counselor—someone who will listen, someone who can help you. Don't suffer alone. And don't blame yourself. You may not be able to change things overnight but at least you'll be getting your feelings out in the open. And that's a lot better than keeping them bottled up inside.

3

My Friends Aren't Always My Friends

Dear Judy,

I'm going to be ten soon. I'm glad I'm writing to you because I really have nobody to talk to. I just lost my best friend. Her name is Carolyn. We used to share secrets, play together and we even had a club! But then Jennifer came along. Jennifer has a clique with some other girls. Me and Carolyn made a vow never to be in that clique because Jennifer, the leader of the pack, tells you what to wear, what to eat, who to like and what labels to buy. But Carolyn went with her anyway and now Carolyn doesn't like me anymore.

I can't talk to my mom about anything private or personal because I'm too embarrassed.

Bonnie, age 10

I had two friends in elementary school, Jane and Rachel. We weren't always kind to each other. Sometimes I was more friendly with one than the other. Sometimes one of us felt left out by the other two. Sometimes jealousies developed.

One afternoon, when I was in sixth grade, Jane's mother came to my house and asked to speak to my mother. Since my mother and Jane's mother were not friends I was surprised. I went outside, and when I returned an hour later, my mother was upset. Jane's mother had told her that Rachel and I had been spreading rumors about Jane. She wanted my mother to put a stop to it. "Children are very cruel," Jane's mother told mine. My mother repeated that phrase several times. *Children are very cruel.* Each time she said it I cringed.

Jane was horrified when she found out that her mother had gone to see my mother. This was not a case of a child being victimized. We were three friends who squabbled regularly and then resolved our own problems.

We can't fight these battles for our kids, nor do they want us to. Sometimes, all we can do is recognize and acknowledge our kids' pain and help them become more aware of others' feelings.

Dear Judy,

I want to discuss my problem with you. One, I've never had a friend, really. The only time I'm popular is when I'm on the school bus because I know good dirty jokes and I shout funny things out the window.

I've got two people who are supposed to be my friends, Elena and Pam. Pam tries to make me jealous for some reason. Elena is too bossy and she's mean to me when someone popular is nice to her.

I have told you this because you write about children and their problems. Do you have any suggestions for me?

Geraldine, age 10

Dear Judy,

I have a problem that many face but most people don't realize it. I am unusually smart for my age (although I don't know why) and because of it I've lost a *lot* of friends. Even my best friend can't (won't) try to understand. She says that now that I'm taking the test into college I won't want to hang around her. But that's not true! I would give up my education and the ability to be smart if I could have a *real* best friend who will accept *me* for what I am. Do you think I'm asking for too much?

Brooke, age 13

As long as kids have a friend they seem able to handle anything. But when they feel different, like Brooke, or when their friends feel threatened by their difference, the friendship is in jeopardy. When kids don't understand or are envious they often deal with their feelings by lashing out at the one whom they consider different.

I wrote to Brooke about a friend of mine, a writer who struggled for years. While she was struggling her friends were there for her, offering support and understanding. As soon as she made it they began to withdraw, accusing her of thinking she was now too good for them. She was deeply hurt by their reactions to her success. She asked me if I had encountered the same rejection. I told her that to some extent, I had, but eventually I found out who my real friends were.

Brooke's mother gave her *The Gifted Kids Survival Guide,* which helped some, but Brooke was still feeling depressed. Instead of seeing her abilities and talents as a blessing, Brooke saw them as something that separated her from her friends.

Dear Judy,

I am in fourth grade. I wanted to tell you that I have a million problems. My friends always gang up on me. They kicked me out of the play one week before the actual play. They put a new girl in my place. They're always doing things like that to me. They pass dirty notes about me *to me!* They call me bad names and they don't know what they mean. They don't know the difference between *stupid* and *dumb*. They don't even know what a *bitch* is. All of them tell lies.

I have arthritis in my right knee. I play piano and dance. I seem to be a math whiz. I have a bumper which pushes my teeth out. I have a million rashes.

Sometimes my friends come back and want to be friends again, but then, the next day, they just gang up on me like before. What should I do?

Hillary, age 9

Dear Judy,

Please help me with this problem at school. Two kids, Lesley and Donna, are not in a fight with me—it's a feud! It all started after our school play. Donna promised me that I could help her and Lesley pass out flowers to the teachers. Then they did it without me. This made me mad and I yelled at them.

The next day I discovered that all of my old friends were crossing my name off their notebooks. I was horrified. My whole body felt like Jell-O! What had I done to them? Then I thought, It's Donna! And it was. I looked at her and she gave me the eye before putting her hands in front of her face to avoid looking at me. The rest of the day was torture! My class teased me about everything. They called me "Brace Face," "Tinsel Teeth," "the Ratty Redhead," "Ugly," "Grotesque" and more. But what bothered me most is that they pretended to be me by curling their hair around their fingers the way I used to. But I've stopped doing that!

I came home crying and totally miserable. I really wished that I had someone to tell my troubles to. My mother doesn't understand. She says she's sick of this "ganging up" thing, and would I please try to find some new friends. Well, Donna took all my friends away so I tried to talk to my teacher. She said to just ignore them. I tried both ideas for two weeks and they both failed.

I really need help. Last night I was in hysterics. I grabbed at my carpet and screamed very loudly. I thought of running away and also of committing suicide. Sometimes I still feel like doing that. And today was the worst day in my entire life! School was horrible, my sisters and mother wouldn't stop nagging me and I just lay on my bed and screamed. Then I thought of you and I knew you would understand. Please, please help me!

Molly, age 11

Two weeks can seem like an eternity to a child who is suffering. If Molly had had comfort and understanding at home, I think she would have fared better. The reassurance that "this too shall pass" might not have been enough, but it would have been better than the message she got from her family—that no one was really listening to her.

4

My Parents Don't Like My Friends

Dear Judy,
    My name is Jason and I am nine years old. I like your books. I have a lot of problems. Like I have a girlfriend whose name is Anne. My mother thinks that I should have boyfriends instead of girlfriends. What should I do? My life is really down in the pits! I need help.

Jason, age 9

Dear Judy,
    My mother doesn't like my friends. She says they are nothing but trouble. She blames them for every little thing that goes wrong.

Debbie, age 13

Dear Judy,
    My parents are always telling me who my

friends should be. They say things like "How come you're not friends with Carly? She gets good grades and she can play the flute."

Miranda, age 12

Lots of kids complain that their parents want to choose their friends. I know a family who moved cross-country to get their son away from friends whom they considered a bad influence. But their son, Max, got in just as much trouble in the new place. It wasn't so much Max's friends who were the problem. It was Max. When they realized this they got professional help.

A friend of mine, Sherry, absolutely can't stand her teenage daughter's best friend. She refuses to speak to this girl when her daughter, Julie, brings her home. I asked Sherry what she doesn't like about Julie's friend and she said, "I don't like anything!" But her negative comments and behavior put Julie on the defensive. Instead, maybe she should spend some time with Julie's friend and try to get to know her better. Also, if Sherry talked with Julie about her friend, she might find out what the attraction is. In any event, we have to accept the fact that we may not like and approve of all of our children's friends.

5

Overweight and Overwrought

Dear Judy,

My favorite book of yours is *Blubber*. It makes me feel funny because I am on the large side and all my friends say how fat I am and they are all small. What should I do? I am only nine years old and I am in fifth grade. I am always going on diets and nothing ever happens.

Caitlin, age 9

In *Blubber*, Wendy uses Linda's weight as a weapon and teases her about it nonstop.

I was a very skinny kid. Adults were always trying to convince me to eat more. And the harder they tried, the more I resisted. I was told I would get scurvy or rickets. I was told that I was so skinny a bird could blow me away. I was told that I needed more meat on my bones. I dreaded mealtimes. I didn't really enjoy food until I was older, until I understood that I didn't have to finish everything on my plate. That the children who were starving in other parts of the world weren't starving because I couldn't finish my dinner.

I hated being weighed at school because I was so thin. Thin was not "in" when I was growing up. The boys teased me, saying, "If Judy swallowed an olive she'd look pregnant." I can still remember the nurse weighing me and saying, "Not quite fifty yet." I was also short. In school we lined up in size places. I was always first on line, unless we lined up in reverse order, and then I was last. I didn't like being the smallest one in class. I wanted to be round and strong like Nancy, who was always first to be picked for the kickball team. I was picked last. Granted, it is much easier to be thin than to be overweight. But when I was young health was measured by weight and if you didn't weigh enough, according to the charts, then you couldn't be healthy.

My mother was overweight. She was always going on diets. But whenever something was bothering her she ate secretly. Ice cream was her passion. I have a teenage friend who is also a secret eater. She eats when she's feeling bad and then she gets angry with herself. She starts diets, then pigs out with her friends and feels guilty.

Dear Judy,

I am fourteen years old and have been overweight ever since fifth grade and I have to be blunt with you, I'm sick of girls in books describing themselves as slim and pretty with brown eyes. To me that's a put-down. If you wrote a book about an overweight girl with a happy ending, that might encourage girls like me to lose weight.

Boys are another problem. All the ones I know make fun of me. It's really hard. Afterwards I go home and cry or eat. I have three brothers and three sisters. My parents are married and live happily. I'm in ninth grade and will be going into high school next year. That's about it.

Thank you for reading my note. I just thought since you write about serious problems, you might be interested in mine. I just hope this note won't bring you down.

Abigail, age 14

Dear Judy,

I am a fourteen-year-old boy. I can relate to *Blubber* very easily because when I was in grade school I was severely overweight. I had no friends and I was considered a sissy because I didn't like boys' games and I related to the girls. Things have changed. I am now skinny and pretty popular. I wish I would have had your books back then.

Kevin, age 14

Kids: People come in a variety of sizes, shapes and weights. Being very fat or very thin can certainly be a problem in terms of health. But for most people the problem is how they feel about themselves and how others treat them. Some kids develop distorted images of themselves, believing they are overweight when they aren't, and they begin to diet compulsively. That can be very dangerous. If you are concerned about your eating habits or your weight and you want to make some sensible changes, ask your parents or your doctor to help you.

6

Moving Away

Dear Judy,
  My best friend is going to move and I am going to miss her so much! Every night I cry so hard because I will miss her a lot. She is a great friend. Please write and tell me what to do.

Suzanna, age 13

Until I began to work on this section I didn't realize how often I had written about moving in my books. Moving away, being the new kid in school, and having to make new friends must have been an even more important part of my life than I thought.

I grew up living in one house, from the age of two until I went off to college. But during third and fourth grades I spent the better part of the school year in Florida. It was very hard to leave my friends in New Jersey, who had been my friends since preschool. And it was scary to be the new girl in class in Miami Beach.

On my first day of school there one girl came up to me and whispered, "I don't like you and I'm never going to like you." I came home from school crying, sure that I would never find a friend at Central Beach Elementary School.

Recently, a friend asked, "If you could go back and relive one year of your childhood, without being able to make any changes, which year would it be?" Without hesitation I answered, "Fourth grade in Miami Beach," because in Miami Beach I learned to make new friends, I discovered an easygoing lifestyle that I had never known before, and I found out that moving isn't always so bad.

But at the time they are going through it, kids don't always agree. The following two letters are from Katie, who grew up moving back and forth between Korea and America.

Dear Judy,

My big problem is that we might move soon. This time my father has decided to take a new job with a big corporation. I may not go though. I don't want to. School here is so fun! If my parents find out that I don't want to move mainly because of my friends I'll never hear the end of it.

I seem to be falling into a depression. I can't do my homework and my grades are dropping. Sometimes I just shut myself up in my room and write. Oh, I wish we didn't have to move!

Katie, age 11

Dear Judy,

Well, we've moved. I feel absolutely terrible. I've cried three times today. It's all so unfair. My

parents can call anyone or see anyone they like.
Not me! And I doubt they even want to see
anyone as much as I want to see my friends in
Korea. At night I can hear their voices and then,
when I wake up and find out where I am, I feel
like going away. I feel like leaving my family.

I have so many dreams. And every one of them
is about school. Once I dreamed I received a
telegram from them. And another one was about
a school dance. But what's the use of dreaming?
What's the use of screaming my head off? *Nothing!* Because I'm here in America. I'm gone and
will never see my friends again and that's it.

Katie, age 11

Moving was an important part of my children's lives,
too. Until they were eleven and nine we lived in one
house and they attended one elementary school. In the
next six years they attended six different schools, in
New Jersey, England and New Mexico. Each time we
moved they had to make new friends. It wasn't easy.
Randy took her time. She watched and waited and
usually found one close friend. Larry jumped in and
tried to make friends with everyone right away. Now
they tell me they're glad they had the chance to live in
different places. They say it gave them a broader
outlook and a sense of adventure that some of their
friends don't share. But I remember the anxiety of
those moves and the time it took all of us to adjust.

7

An Embarrassing Problem

Dear Judy,
I have an idea for you. It's a problem that I have at school. You see, at school everyone says that I once went in my pants, which is true. But I don't want to admit it. Mandy, this girl in my class, started joking about it. She put water next to my seat and did other things which really hurt my feelings, so when I got home I told my parents everything and cried. Now I hate everyone in my class.

Toby, age 10

When I returned from Miami Beach, at the beginning of fifth grade, there was a new girl in my class. She had moved to our neighborhood while I was away. Her name was Diane and everyone said that she wet her pants. While I never saw this happen I joined my classmates when they held their noses and said "P.U."

as Diane walked by. And when someone poured a cup of water next to Diane's desk, making it look as if the puddle on the floor was her fault, I laughed with everyone else. Maybe Diane did have a problem. I don't know. I think she probably had one accident and the kids in our class weren't going to let her forget it.

At the end of fifth grade I went away to summer camp for the first time. One night, at camp, I had a vivid dream. In my dream I saw myself get out of bed, walk to the toilet, sit down, and pee. When I awoke I found that I had wet my bed. I was horrified. I didn't know what to do. We had a bed wetter in our bunk, Rebecca, and everyone made fun of her. This had never happened to me before. I was humiliated.

As I lay awake at dawn, I tried to figure out what to do. I thought about turning my dream into a joke, saying, "Ha ha . . . look what happened to me during the night." But I was afraid to take that chance. So I got up in the morning and made my bed, with the wet and smelly sheets, as if nothing had happened. I slept on those sheets for the rest of the week. I guess the others assumed the smell was coming from Rebecca's bed since her bed was next to mine. By laundry day my sheets were dry. I stuffed them into the laundry bag and never mentioned the incident to anyone.

That never happened to me again, but it was an experience I will never forget. If my bunkmates at camp had found out my secret they might have teased me the same way my classmates at school teased Diane. I wish now that I had been brave enough to be honest about what had happened. Maybe they would have understood after all. Maybe we all could have laughed together. But at eleven, I could not risk it.

Dear Judy,

I'm fourteen years old, a boy, and going into ninth grade in the fall. I've enjoyed reading your books because they talk about kids' problems, like other books don't, from a kid's point of view.

I have a problem that I've never seen a kids' book about. I bet thousands of kids my age who have my problem would like it if you wrote a book about this problem because if you did, we would feel less bad about it.

My problem is I still wet the bed. I've been a bed wetter as long as I can remember. No one except my family knows about it and I'm scared to death that someone will find out. My mom doesn't say much when I wet the bed but I know that she's tired of washing sheets and pajamas every morning and wishes I would stop. I have two younger sisters and an older brother. None of them say anything about my bed-wetting mainly because my mom told them if they ever tell anyone they'll get punished bad. But I know that they laugh when they see Mom washing my sheets.

If I ever want to sleep over anywhere I have to make sure no one finds out I still wet the bed. So I have to swallow my pride and wear two diapers and a pair of rubber pants. I have to make sure that nobody sees them in the luggage or sees me putting them into a plastic bag in the morning. I don't sleep over much because the worrying I do about being found out is more than the fun of sleeping over.

My doctor gave me medicine but it didn't help. I tried a bed-wetting alarm but it woke up everybody but me. Not taking liquids before bedtime didn't help either. I feel like a baby but I can't help it because it happens when I'm sleeping.

I hear a lot of kids making fun of kids they know that wet the bed and maybe if you wrote a book those kids would know that it's nothing to make fun of. I know me and other kids who wet the bed would feel a lot better too.

Thanks.

Gary, age 14

Experts tell me that 7 percent of all males still wet the bed at age seven, and that the problem persists for 2 percent at age eighteen. If your teenager is a bed-wetter ask your family physician for advice. He or she might refer you to a urologist. Bed-wetting can also be caused by psychological problems. Discuss this possibility with your doctor, too. A consultation with a psychiatrist or psychologist may be appropriate.

Dear Judy,

I am twelve and have a problem. You see, I have a friend, Kim, that nobody else likes. She's very nice but when she laughs she pees in her pants. Well, she wants to laugh and have some fun but people just don't understand. If I go around with her the others don't like me. If I go around without her then she feels sad. Maybe you're going to say that the others aren't very good friends, but that's an adult point of view. We are only eleven and twelve years old.

Sometimes I do feel like pushing the others in a mud puddle. I want to be everyone's friend but the others snob me off and give me dirty looks. Oh, I wish they would grow up!

I have talked to the school counselor and he wasn't any help. My mom suggested I write to you. Help, please!

Sandy, age 12

Sandy has found out earlier than most kids that often we have to make the toughest decisions on our own. We all need to be reminded that we can't have a close friend without being one too.

Chapter III

I AM JUST LIKE EVERYONE ELSE, EXCEPT . . .

1

I Am Disabled

Dear Judy,
  I am fourteen years old and I have cerebral palsy and writing helps me to understand some of life's situations. But I wish you would write a book explaining what it's like so others would understand me.

Claire, age 14

Almost all the letters in this chapter are from young people asking me to write a book about someone with their disability or illness. These kids aren't looking for sympathy. They just want other kids and adults to understand what their problem means and that aside from that problem they are just like everyone else.

When I was growing up my friend, Marcia, had a cousin who had cerebral palsy. Her name was Joan and she was a few years older than we were. When she visited Marcia's family we were expected to include her in our play. We knew that Joan was different from other kids—her speech was slurred, making it difficult to understand what she was saying and her coordination was not good—but we did not know what made her different. We were uncomfortable around her but no one ever explained her disability to us. No one ever sat us down and said, "Joan has cerebral palsy. Inside, she is just like everyone else. Just like you and your friends. She has the same feelings and the same needs." Adults sometimes whispered about such problems but never so the kids could hear. We were unaware then and we were kept unaware because of our parents' discomfort.

I wish I could tell Joan, now that I am grown up I understand. I wish I could tell her about Philip, who taught me, in a few minutes and a few letters, what being disabled can mean.

I met Philip in a bookstore, in Yonkers, New York. Both he and his older brother were in wheelchairs, accompanied by their younger brother, who is not disabled, and their mother. For a moment I didn't know what to say, but once Philip began to talk he was so full of life, so full of good humor, he put me at ease immediately. He told me that he had muscular dystrophy. After our meeting he wrote to me.

Dear Judy,

You may not remember me. You met me when you were in Yonkers, New York, when you were signing autographs for your new book. I was the person in a wheelchair who asked you if I could be a model for a book about a boy like me. I am twelve years old and I have a fourteen-year-old brother and a seven-year-old brother who is the wildest thing in the world. My older brother is also in a wheelchair.

The main feature of the story I want to tell is that a disabled twelve-year-old boy is no different from any other twelve-year-old boy even though he has to do some things in a different way because of his disability. I want to tell everyone about my school days (I am in a regular seventh grade class, not a special class with only disabled kids), my camping trips (I have camped all over the U.S.—well, almost all over), how I get hassled by my mother and have brother troubles like any other kid my age.

When kids meet me for the first time they are puzzled about my wheelchair and if they're not too shy they ask me lots of questions about how I do things, including even how I go to the bathroom! (When I was in kindergarten someone asked me if I turned my wheelchair upside down on top of me so I could lie on my bed at night. He thought it was permanently attached!) When they ask me things like that I wonder if all their smarts went out of their heads.

That's why I think this book needs to be written. It will help to answer all those dumb questions and will help kids like me to show we really are mostly like the rest of the guys.

Philip, age 12

I encouraged Philip to write that book himself. I really believed that someday he would. It never occurred to me that there wouldn't be time. I regret the moments I could have shared with Philip. I regret the chance I missed to really know him and to help him tell his story so that the world could know him too. I didn't understand how frail he was. I didn't know he would not live. Philip died two years later. He was fourteen years old.

Dear Judy,

My name is Sonya. I am fifteen years old. I am deaf but I can talk and hear some. I would be glad if you would write three stories. Let me tell you what they would be about:

1. This story would be about a pretty girl who was deaf and so lonely. She needs someone to be with. She has some girlfriends but she needs to be loved by a boyfriend, too. No one thinks about deaf people having normal boyfriends and girl-friends.

2. This is about how a popular boy falls in love with a deaf girl. Many girls who are madly in love with the most popular boy in school wonder why he would fall in love with her. The other girls tell the deaf girl he doesn't really like her because she is deaf. The deaf girl feels very hurt. But he really does like her. No one knows this until later.

3. This story is about a deaf girl and her normal mother. The deaf girl is smart but her mother calls her stupid and when she does she hurts the girl's feelings. So the girl yells back, "Why don't you call yourself stupid!"

I am sure that people would like these stories and they would understand how this girl feels.

I was born deaf because my mother got German measles when she was pregnant. My parents found out I couldn't hear when I was a few months old.

Sonya, age 15

Dear Judy,

I am a fourteen-year-old girl and everyone at this age has problems. But I have one problem that most teenagers don't have. My problem doesn't have a name so I don't know what to call it. Have you heard of being so angry you could pull out your hair? Well, that's what I do, not only because I am angry but also because I get very nervous.

I live in Chicago, which has a high crime rate. I don't like it when my parents or my older brother stay out late. I live in a little suburb but my parents go out to the city and other places and I worry about them. Also, I have a sister just one year younger than me who gets me angry. She is pretty, has more friends and is smarter than me, though we're both in advanced classes. I'm not ugly but because of my hair I don't look too great. I have many other reasons for my problem but these two are the main ones.

A dermatologist told me that this would take three years to overcome and that many kids have this problem. I started in the middle of sixth grade so my three years are almost up. I know two other girls who have had this problem. Dana had this problem when she was in fifth and sixth grades. Her parents put a lot of pressure on her because she was very talented. Now Dana has overcome her hair problems but not her parent problem and she takes drugs and has wasted her life. Terry has this problem because of her older sister who is brilliant. Both Terry and Dana went almost totally bald. Dana has grown back her hair but Terry is still working on it, like me. My hair is only thin on top so I guess you could say I went half bald.

Dana told people that she had a disease but I've just made up excuses like, I accidentally cut my hair. I've only told my best friend because if I told anyone else they would think I was a freak. Terry, though, will tell anyone that asks her that she pulls her hair out. No one seems to mind but I haven't got that much courage.

Nicole, age 14

I feel very fortunate that I have never experienced anything as serious as the disabilities or illnesses discussed in this chapter, either firsthand or through my kids. But the chronic eczema I had during my childhood and early adolescence taught me that not all illnesses and disabilities are physical. Some are emotional, some are a combination.

When I was in seventh grade I had a strong allergic reaction to the standard salve which was used to treat eczema. This "flare-up," as the doctors called it, caused a disfiguring rash that covered my whole body. My face swelled and my eyes shut. My parents took me to a specialist in New York. When he first saw me he asked them if I had ever had normal skin. When I heard that I began to cry. I felt very sorry for myself. The doctor wanted to put me in the hospital until my condition was under control but I begged him to let me stay at home. So my mother drove me to New York every day for two weeks, where I was given a new cortisone drug.

In a few months I was fine. The rash and the swelling disappeared, although I was supposed to wear white cotton gloves to bed each night, so that if I did scratch in my sleep I would not do much damage.

Nine years later, when my father died, I had another "flare-up." It took me a long time to really understand that for me, emotional distress and physical symptoms are closely related.

Dear Judy,

You have written many books on problems that children face in everyday life. But you haven't written a book on dyslexia. Dyslexia is not a disease. It is a brain slip that occurs mostly in left-handers, mostly males, but in one out of ten cases, in females. Dyslexics have trouble in reading, spelling and in math.

Bruce Jenner has it and Albert Einstein had it. Some people think it is a form of retardation. It isn't. It is a learning disability. Dyslexics can be very bright.

I have dyslexia and I am also short, only four feet ten inches. Sometimes, in school, dyslexics are put into special classes. We are called dummies and that hurts. School is very hard for a dyslexic person. They may get hyperactive and show their anger and frustration by throwing things.

I hope you will consider writing a book on this. I would appreciate it and more people and kids will understand dyslexia then.

Iris, age 12

2

I Have a Serious Illness

Dear Judy,

I read a lot but I haven't found any books—good enough to be believed—that are about a preteen girl going through a bad problem: cancer and the amputation of a lower leg. I went through this myself. I would sometimes like everyone to know just how much this thing hurts, especially chemotherapy. First you lose a limb, then your hair. Maybe those who make fun should go through it themselves. I know quite well that good writing depends upon experience but I have a feeling that somehow you could do it.

Chrissy, age 12

Dear Judy,

I'm eleven years old and I'm an asthmatic. Could you write a book about an asthmatic who does really well in drawing? If you do, please stress that we aren't freaks and that we can be more than bench warmers. We can even have girlfriends!

Arthur, age 11

Dear Judy,
   I'll be seventeen in July. I am writing to ask you if you would write my story. You probably think that there isn't much story behind a sixteen-year-old's life. You're wrong.
   There is a big story behind eleven of my sixteen years. You see, I am an asthmatic. Speaking from personal experience, every attack is a new and unexplored feeling. There are a lot of emotional facets in dealing with asthma. Some of them are—feelings about being a whole person, normality and being diseased. A stronger emotion deals with death. There are no books I can find about the feelings which asthmatics have about themselves and the others that surround them. I think a book would help a lot of people understand asthma and the feelings surrounding it better.

Sharon, age 16

Dear Judy,
   I have a suggestion for a book. The suggestion is—why not write a book on a diabetic. A few months ago I found out I am a diabetic. It was pretty scary to find out. I was horrified to learn that it is a major killer and attacks more than two percent of the world's population.
   I'm doing fine now. I play baseball (I'm a

pitcher) and I'm doing much better in school. I'm in sixth grade.

Robyn, age 11

Dear Judy,
  I am a ten-year-old girl with a problem. I've got diabetes. I just found out about it this Easter. It seems like every time I get sick it's on a holiday or vacation. I have been in the hospital four times. Once on Easter and another time on Halloween. I also have asthma. I think it would be nice if you would write about a little girl with diabetes. I would be glad to share my experiences with you. This past year I won the county spelling bee.

Bridget, age 10

Dear Judy,
  Last summer I was diagnosed with myasthenia gravis, otherwise known as M.G. It is a neuro-muscular disease. I have to take prednisone which swells up my cheeks. Kids think I'm just plain fat, but I'm not. It's my cheeks, that's all. But kids seem to like calling me "Fat" or "Fat with Four Eyes." Plus, on top of all that, I have allergies to everything from trees to peanuts.
  I can just feel that this new year is going to be the same as the last one. How do you think I can prevent it from happening again?
  Oh, I forgot to tell you that I love to dance. I mean *really* dance. I'm not your everyday dancing student. I am pretty good.

Heidi, age 11

78

Dear Judy,

When and if you ever write another book I have a subject you may be interested in. It's called cystic fibrosis (C.F.). It affects the respiratory and digestive systems. Me and a bunch of my other friends could be your reference sources since we suffer from it. You could mix facts with the character's personality. I think that is important in a good book.

Anyhow, it's something to think about. You see, almost nobody knows about C.F. so when I tell my "friends" about it they no longer want to be my "friends." I think (though I'm not positive) that they're scared off because of common ignorance of the whole disease. They're simply afraid of what they don't know and it makes me sick! In fact, so few people know about it it's called the "silent disease."

Olivia, age 12

Kids often taunt each other out of ignorance. They are curious but afraid to ask questions. The best way to help them get comfortable is by talking with them. Knowledge leads to understanding. Once there is some understanding kids can get past their own fears and become friends. But adults have to be there to help present the facts. If your kids are older you might read up on the subject together, then talk about what it would mean to have such a problem.

My friend's son, Seth, began to have seizures when he was fourteen. Sometimes he had seizures at school. The other kids gave him a hard time. Even some of his teachers shunned him. They let him know that he was no longer welcome on school trips or at athletic events.

These teachers and students didn't bother to get the facts about Seth's problem. They were reacting to their own fears.

But suppose someone—a teacher, the school nurse, a parent, a doctor—had come to the school and, with Seth's permission, had explained why and how Seth's brain triggered these seizures, and what to do in case Seth had one in class or while he was out with his friends? Suppose the kids had been encouraged to ask questions? Suppose Seth helped too, by sharing some of his feelings and fears with his classmates? I believe that would have changed the picture.

I know kids don't want to call attention to their differences. I know I am talking about some very complicated feelings and there is no way it is going to be easy, not for the child, not for the family of the child, not for the friends or the teachers. But pretending that there is no problem doesn't help either.

I have a friend who has epilepsy. I asked him what to do in case he ever had a seizure while I was with him. He explained. I felt reassured. Kids also need that kind of reassurance.

Dear Judy,

I have scoliosis and have been in a brace for a year now. When I first got my brace I was told I would have to wear it for two years. I felt just like Deenie, in your book, very embarrassed.

I cried when I had to start high school. The first few weeks I could hear people whispering about me. I felt like walking out of class and one time I almost did. Then I began to make friends. Things began to work very well and I found out something very important. *The kids just wanted to know what my brace was for.*

I also thought that no boys would ever talk to me but I was wrong. They didn't seem to mind at all. They were curious too, just like everyone else. Now when people stare at me I don't mind because it doesn't bother me at all.

Audrey, age 15

In 1970 I met Wendy, a fourteen-year-old girl with scoliosis, a curvature of the spine. The treatment for scoliosis varies from back braces, sometimes worn for three or four years, to surgery. Wendy wore a Milwaukee Brace. She was very open about her problem and shared some of her feelings and experiences with me. Her mother was having a harder time adjusting to the situation than Wendy. Wendy inspired me to write the book *Deenie,* about a young girl with scoliosis. Even though Deenie's disability is temporary and correctable, it affects the way she sees herself and it affects the way her family and friends see her and treat her. Because of the book *Deenie* I have received hundreds of letters from young people with scoliosis.

Dear Judy,

I recently found out I have scoliosis. So I read your book *Deenie* over again. It helped me cope with the hard times. I felt I could really relate to the character—the problems, anger and confusion, the frustration, embarrassment, questions, worry.

The only difference is, I had the operation. I'm now lying in bed for five months in a body cast and then I have to wear a walking cast for another two months. I'm thinking of using Deenie's line about jumping off the Empire State Building, when people ask questions. It's easier than explaining.

Tina, age 13

Dear Judy,

Very shortly ago I received news that I had scoliosis. It happened like this: I'm in the fifth grade and the district was having a screening for fifth through eighth graders. The screening was for scoliosis. All the girls went down to the music room (the boys went to the gym). I was almost last to go in. A lot of girls came out looking worried after their turn. Then I found out why. Our school nurse is very cold. She never seems to explain anything. When it was my turn all she said to me was, "Come back Monday, please." I went out and talked to Iris who was now crying. She said that the nurse told her to come back Monday, too. Later we found out that four more girls had to come back on Monday.

On Monday I was last to go in. All the other girls were okay. But when my mother got home that day she told me the nurse had called her at work and told her to take me to the doctor. A few days later we went to see him. Sure enough, I had scoliosis. So we made an appointment with a specialist. A few days after that I went to the library and as I was leaving I saw this book by you, *Deenie.* I checked it out. Later I found out it was a book about a girl with scoliosis. I really enjoyed it. Your book comforted me.

Jody, age 11

Dear Judy,

Hi, remember me? I'm Isabel. I'm the one who has scoliosis. It's very embarrassing wearing a brace. Every time I go through a bomb detector at an airport I set it off. In the summertime it is very sticky and sweaty. In my school I am the only one who wears a brace. I feel so funny wearing it. It feels like I'm the only one in the world who does, but I know I'm not. It's hard to bend down. My face turns all red and I look like a tomato. In my school they're having a scoliosis screening. They make you bend over to see if you have it.

I think my name, Isabel, is very boring. My father's mother's name was Isabel so I got stuck with it. I would rather be called Amy or Antonia. If my name was Antonia I could be called Toni. I like that name.

I like sports. I like swimming, running, tennis, basketball and softball. I want to be an actress. I want to be really famous. My face is okay, my stomach is so-so, my legs are yuck (so long and gross) and my feet are huge. I have bigger feet than my mother. I take a size 9. I feel like a gorilla. I'm going to be twelve soon and haven't had my period yet. I'm waiting. I don't have too much up front, but I hope I'll get something.

What a dreamer I am. I'll probably grow up to work in a bank!

Isabel, age 11

Most kids who write to me about scoliosis have adjusted remarkably well. Some disabilities and illnesses are permanent. Scoliosis patients know that with treatment, their condition is correctable. Still, I include the following letter, from Nancy, because there may be other young people who are struggling, the way she did. Nancy was twenty-seven when she wrote to me.

Dear Judy,

Recently I read *Deenie* and I can't begin to tell you how it touched me—in my heart, in my stomach and in my head. *Deenie* opened up an old, apparently still unhealed wound, well-hidden, but festering nonetheless.

When I was eleven, I was a Deenie—but without the benefit of a friend or a loving father. What Deenie went through was almost identical to my thoughts, feelings and reactions, except mine, for whatever reason, seem to have been more magnified, more intense, and much longer lasting.

I'm twenty-seven now. I was sixteen when I got out of the brace. When I was eighteen I began having anxiety-panic attacks and was terrified. I went to a therapist.

Within the first few months of therapy, something about my scoliosis slipped out. I hadn't kept it a secret. It was just something in the past, I thought, and no longer a part of my life. But the brace had played a tremendous, critical role in my social and psychological development. While it may have straightened my back, it crippled the rest of me.

During therapy my therapist had me get the damned brace, which was in a green trash bag in a corner of my bedroom closet (the orthopedist thought I might need it again) and throw it out.

Deenie stirred up a lot of things in me. Some things I'd forgotten suddenly came back. I started to read up on current treatment for scoliosis. Today patients are able to take the brace off for half-hour periods during the day. They can stand up without wearing it and can take a bath or shower. When I wore the brace I wasn't allowed to stand up without it. It had to be put on and taken off while I was lying down. This left me with the idea that if I stood or sat up without the brace my spine would collapse or whatever correction had been achieved would be lost in seconds. It also meant I was restricted to sponge baths which were humiliating, and left me helpless in the hands of a bitchy, neurotic, overprotective mother. The issue of dependence on others doesn't seem to have been raised in the articles I've read so far.

I still wonder how Deenie's dad was able to hug her. Did he have very long arms, or didn't Deenie's brace stick out as much as mine or was it that Deenie could feel her father's touch on the sides of her arms? Nobody could hug me during my years in the brace except my dog, Rusty. She managed to love me no matter what and her love saved me. She came into my life just before I got the brace and she kept me from committing suicide.

Nancy, age 27

No one ever talked with Nancy about her scoliosis. No one explained to her exactly what was happening. I think her doctor was at fault for leaving her with those false and scary impressions. Probably she didn't ask questions and neither did her parents. Nancy might have had emotional problems anyway, but the way her family handled her scoliosis made the situation worse.

The kids who write to me about scoliosis have more information than Nancy had. And there have been a lot of changes in the treatment of scoliosis since Nancy was eleven. Today, scoliosis patients can swim and exercise and bathe.

I really feel for Nancy and what she went through— five years of sponge baths with her mother's assistance during the very years her body was changing, when she needed the most privacy. And it never occurred to me, until I read her letter, that no one could hug a person wearing a brace. There are so many ways to hug, to show affection. I hate to think that other kids are going through what Nancy did, without a supportive family and without information. Again, what kids imagine is usually worse than the truth, so instead of hiding the facts from them, talk to them. Share your feelings and encourage them to share theirs. And remind them that curiosity should not be mistaken for lack of sensitivity.

Chapter IV
WHEN YOUR WORLD IS TURNING TOPSY-TURVY

1

Splitting Up

Dear Judy,

I am eight years old and have a problem. My mom and dad aren't split up but they are always fighting and it's a scary feeling to think that someday they are going to get divorced. Sometimes I just want to yell out, "Stop fighting!" But I can't. Please help.

Sarah, age 8

Divorce is so common in today's world that kids are frightened when their parents fight or even disagree. This is it, they think, the end of our family!

When my children were young we lived in a suburban New Jersey neighborhood, and as family after family split up my kids became fearful that this could happen to us, too. I tried to reassure them but I wasn't really sure myself. I wrote *It's Not the End of the World* at that time, to try to answer some of my children's questions about divorce, to let other kids know they were not alone and, perhaps, because I was not happy in my marriage. I kept those feelings deep inside. For years I would not, could not, admit that we had any problems. The perfect daughter had become the perfect wife and mother.

Working on this chapter has been very difficult for me because if I am to be honest then I have to write about the worst years of my life and the mistakes I made.

John and I had been married for sixteen years (our children were fourteen and twelve) when we split up. The next years were more stressful, more painful, more threatening than anything I had ever experienced. That we survived reasonably intact says a lot for the strength of family love, for the ability of children to cope and for how basically decent people can hurt each other terribly, come close to the breaking point, then pull themselves back together again.

Dear Judy,

After one month of constant fighting between my parents (and them not sleeping in the same bed and not eating dinner together) my mom finally said, "I want a divorce."

I've learned to get along without my father at home. I get to see him quite often but I still miss him very much. Your book, *It's Not the End of the World* helped me finally to accept the fact that I could not do anything about my parents' divorce. Well, it's all quiet now except my little sister still cries, "I miss Daddy . . ." all night long.

Paula, age 12

Dear Judy,

My parents just got a divorce and I don't know how to cope with it. I have lots of things on my mind that are bothering me. I don't have anyone to tell them to. If I tell my friends they will tell everyone what I said. I can't tell my mom because she will criticize me and my dad doesn't understand.

Julie, age 11

Dear Judy,

My mom and dad got divorced almost two years ago. I see my dad a lot, at least two times a week. But sometimes I wonder why they got divorced. I kind of know, but I'm not exactly sure.

Dawn, age 12

Before John and I told our kids that we were splitting up, I had a session with a family counselor. She said, "The children will ask you why . . . and you better have some answers." It is much harder for children to understand why their parents are splitting up when there hasn't been any fighting, when either one or both parents have been keeping their feelings of unhappiness, resentment, disappointment and anger inside. It's hard to explain to your kids why this has become an intolerable situation for you. I don't think I was able to do a very good job of it then.

Dear Judy,

I know you get thousands of letters but it would really make me feel good if you would read this one. I'm writing to you about one of my problems. My mom and dad are getting a divorce.

I'm really sad about it, but I wouldn't be so sad if my mom wanted the divorce. See, my dad left us. He left us with not much money. My mom thinks that she is going to have a nervous breakdown and die. She keeps on saying this and it's really making me sick. When this first happened my mom had to go to a hospital for people who are in shock.

It would really help if you would become a friend of mine and write back to me.

Nora, age 11

At the very time my children needed me most, I was least able to give to them. Even though I wanted the divorce it was a time of shock, hurt, anger, sadness and depression.

Just getting through the day was a real struggle for me. I woke up crying every morning and I went to bed crying every night. I wasn't sure I could cope. I had very little left over for my kids. And they were having their own problems. Larry was acting out his feelings. Randy reversed roles with me, becoming the grown-up at fourteen, to the child I had become, at thirty-seven.

What can you do if you find yourself in this position? Be aware! Acknowledge your feelings. Try to remember how frightening a time this is for your kids. Above all, don't try to get through it alone. Get help for yourself and your kids and stick with it.

One of my mistakes was in not being honest with the

family counselor I was seeing right after my divorce. Even at her office, during my weekly sessions, I still pretended that I could handle anything, that my children would be fine, that we didn't have serious problems. I don't know whether she believed me or not. If she did, I guess she wasn't the best counselor for me. But if you don't *want* to face the facts, no one can help you. All I wanted was confirmation that I was okay and that the plans I was making were okay. I wish now that she had forced me to confront my real feelings. I wish that she had been able to prevent me from jumping from the frying pan into the fire. Because that's exactly what I did. Within months I married the first man who came along and I believed that I had her blessing.

I told myself that I knew how to be married, that I was good at being married, that once we were settled the kids would be fine. I told myself a pack of lies because I was terrified at the idea of being alone. I had married John at twenty-one, following my junior year of college. I had never been on my own. What did I know about life? What did I really know about myself? Not much.

Dear Judy,

I was eight years old when my parents were divorced and things have been unfair to me. I didn't know of any *real* arguments or fights between my parents when I was that age. They did have a little spat every now and then, but no real serious fights, at least not around me. Then all of a sudden, I came home from school one day and my mother's clothes were not in the closet. It looked as if she had just moved out. Little did I know, but she had. I was terribly frightened and the whole story brings tears to my eyes just to think about it. I finally found out later, that my mother was at her best friend's house and we went to stay with her until the divorce.

I have felt two-faced for four years. When I come home from being with my father I have to adjust myself to a whole new way of life. Living with my mother is so much different from spending a weekend with my father. Things are so much more pleasant with my father than with my mother.

For most of my life I have been very creative. Before the divorce I could look at a picture and sit down and write a story about it. Now when I go to put what I have in my mind on paper it all goes away. Why?

I am in desperate need of help, not only because of the divorce. Do you understand? Please write me back. And remember, I am writing you this letter in need of a friend, not a famous writer.

Candace, age 11

When John and I first split up the kids would visit him on weekends. He took them to expensive restaurants and to see plays and movies. He entertained them lavishly, not to compete with me, but because he didn't know what else to do. He wanted to show them that he cared, that he loved them, and extravagant weekends were the only way he knew how to do that.

After a while it got to be such a strain on him that he came full circle. He would not entertain them at all. No more plays. No more fancy restaurants. At first Randy and Larry were disappointed. It took years to get it worked out so that they were comfortable together, so that they did not expect to be entertained nonstop when they were with him, and for him to see that it was okay to take them out sometimes, just because he felt like it.

Most kids long for a natural relationship with both parents. There is no doubt that the parent with whom the kids share their daily lives has a different relationship with them than the parent they see only once a week or once a month or whenever. It's up to you, if you're not the everyday parent, to keep your relationship with your kids alive and intimate. Pick up the phone and talk with them often. If you're far away, write to them. And don't let your feelings about the divorce get in the way of your feelings for your kids.

Kids: Remember, during and after a divorce, your parents are suffering too. That doesn't make it any easier, I know, but it's a fact. It's very hard in the beginning, especially if your parents are fighting and you feel caught in the middle, to keep your relationship with both parents going strong. It's okay for you to tell them you're not taking sides, that you're staying out of the fighting and that you don't want to hear anything bad from either parent about the other. Randy learned to say to me, "I don't want to hear about it! That's your problem. You work it out yourself." And she was right. It was my problem, not hers. She wasn't divorcing either one of her parents. There may be times when you will have to remind your parents that this is their divorce, not yours. And that you still love both of them.

Dear Judy,

My name is Lori. I am fourteen years old. I would like to ask you a question if I may. My parents are separated for one year and four months. I live with my father and I'm very happy about living with him. I was also close to my mother but since I faded from my mother's life I got closer to my father. I just wanted to know why I feel that way.

Lori, age 14

Dear Judy,

I am from the fifth grade. My parents are divorced. My mother wants to move to California now but I'm frightened to leave my father. Help!

Yvette, age 10

Dear Judy,

My name is Debbie. You understand how I feel, by what you say in your books. I read that you were very close to your father. So was I, until they got a divorce. Now he lives in Oklahoma and I see him just one time a year. I miss him so much!

Debbie, age 10

When I wrote back to Debbie I said that I hoped her father knew how much she missed him. Once a year is very little time to spend with someone you love. Help your kids understand that just because you don't see each other very often doesn't mean you don't love each other as much. Encourage them to share the everyday adventures of their lives. Sharing details keeps people close. Debbie's father is lucky to have such a loving daughter.

Dear Judy,

Would you do me a favor and write a book about my sort of problems. One is my housekeeper. She's always nagging me to do things. Another is my mom. She's away too often since my parents were divorced. She has to have a really good job but that really good job means she has to go away on business trips a lot. She'll stay at home with me and our housekeeper for a couple of weeks, then she goes on a business trip again.

Another problem is my dad. He drinks too much. I can't go anywhere with him because mom says she doesn't trust him.

Jenny, age 10

Years ago I had a letter from a woman who was en route to Israel. She had left her husband and three children, her beautiful house, her live-in housekeeper, her life. She was running away to begin a new life. The letter was very long and full of emotion. She felt especially guilty about leaving her twelve-year-old daughter, a sensitive child who liked my books. She begged me to write to this child, to try to help her through the difficult times ahead. She hoped I would ease her guilt feelings, encourage her to make a new life and explain what she could not to her daughter. But

I could not explain. I've often thought about that family. I've wondered what happened to them.

In a recent article in the *New York Times* education supplement, called "Youth Hasn't Changed, Society Has," Gisha Berkowitz asks, "How important is algebra if you've just overheard your parents' final quarrel before one of them leaves for good?"

Her plea is for the "schools to be the stable setting in which young people interface with caring adults and social systems and services to help them."

We *do* need to let kids know where they can go for help, and schools could certainly make them aware of community services. Many kids don't know how to ask for help. Many don't even know it's possible. Teachers have to be aware of family situations. Parents should notify schools of family crises. There is no way to separate a child's life and performance in school from what is going on at home.

Dear Judy,
   I am in fifth grade. My parents are divorced. My mom lives in North Carolina and my dad lives in Georgia. I have to see one of them in the summer, depending on who I am living with the rest of the year. I feel very bad about not getting to see both of them all the time. Please write and tell me how your kids felt when you got divorced and they couldn't see their dad all the time.

Roger, age 10

I can't tell Roger how my children felt. Only they could do that. I do think it's easier on kids when their parents stay in the same town and they can freely visit back and forth. That is, if the parents aren't fighting all the time, making visits stressful.

I moved, with my children, to England, just six months after John and I had split up. I thought I was in love and the man that I was marrying had a temporary job in London. I welcomed the opportunity to get away from my mother and her expectations, from John and the power I believed he had over me, and from a life that had become too familiar. I yearned for adventure, for experience, but I didn't know how to find it on my own.

We went to London for just one school semester. I tried to convey my enthusiasm to my kids. I told them that this would be a wonderful experience for them, that we would travel all over Europe together, and that this would be the beginning of a long and happy new marriage for me.

But before long it became clear that this hasty new marriage wasn't going to work and I didn't know what to do about it or how to get out of it without looking like a fool, to John, to my children, to my mother, to the world. From the beginning we fought. We fought, I think, because we didn't take the time to get to know each other. Each of us had invented the person of our dreams and then we were disappointed when we turned out not to be.

After our semester in London we moved to New Mexico, where my new husband had accepted a job. I thought that once we were settled everything might fall into place.

I have to remind myself that even though the next three years were the most difficult of my life, there were good moments. Away from home for the first time, I began to grow up, to sort out my life and the decisions I had made. And there was never a time when I was unable to write. I think writing saved me.

Dear Judy,

I am thirteen and in seventh grade. My parents have been divorced for six years and your book *It's Not the End of the World* is such a coincidence! I have a little sister who is eight and an older brother who is sixteen. My brother lives with my father now but my parents are always going to court and my mother always comes home sad and crying and it scares me.

Marlo, age 13

Dear Judy,

A court fight has been brewing between my ex-wife and me about how much time the kids should spend with me. We have joint custody but I see them only every other weekend. I thought that your book *Smart Women* might give me some insight that would help me in the fight. About halfway through the book, I came to a passage in which Michelle, seventeen, is reflecting on her visit with her father, Freddy.

During Christmas vacation one of Freddy's friends had come over to visit. He had three messed up teenagers from his first marriage but now he was married again and his new wife was pregnant.

"This time I'm going to do it right," he'd told Freddy. "I know a lot more about raising kids now. Forget the permissive stuff. What they need is authority!"

Bull . . . Michelle thought.
What they need is love.

I thought about that line—"What they need is love"—and then I phoned my ex-wife and called off the fight.

Thanks for the insight and thanks too for the plug for divorced fathers. We needed that!

Richard, adult

John and I never had a custody fight or problems about visits. We agreed that Randy and Larry would live with me but would be free to spend as much time as they wanted with him. Because we lived in New Mexico and he lived in New York that meant the kids spent most school holidays and part of every summer with him. He also visited with them in New Mexico once a year so that he could see their home and their school, and meet their friends. He spoke with them on the phone once a week from New York. As they grew older and went off to college they decided where they wanted to spend their holidays. It was never a question of choosing one parent over the other. The decision was based on where their friends and activities took them. John and I made a million mistakes following our divorce but we tried not to use the kids as weapons in our private war. Still, we hurt them by our monthly battles over money and power.

I guess this is the time to say that ours would have been a different story if we had had very little money. By the time we were divorced I was earning a respectable living, and with John's child-support checks we had no financial worries. A few years after that I was earning enough so that money should no longer have been an issue.

I know, from the letters I have received, that divorce for women who have no means of support, except the checks that their ex-husbands may or may not send regularly, and which may not even be enough to feed and clothe the children, let alone pay the rent, is a very different kind of nightmare for a family.

I don't know anyone who has gone through divorce proceedings without bitter arguments over money, whether they are wealthy or poor. John and I fought over who should pay for what because the anger we still felt toward each other was acute. When the old wounds began to heal, when we finally agreed to share all the children's expenses, fifty-fifty (because we could afford to), the air cleared. We were finally able to make peace, even to remember why we had liked each other in the first place. That took five years.

2

The New Person in Mom or Dad's Life

Dear Judy,

My mom and dad are getting divorced and I just got over the chicken pox so my summer hasn't been so great so far. I wrote you before and told you my parents were having trouble and you gave me a little advice to try not to worry too much. Well, now I'm really worried. I keep wondering how me, my mom and my little sister are going to manage on our own. My mom doesn't have a job and she is going to have a hard time trying to find one.

Right now I hate my dad! I know I shouldn't. But I really hate him and I don't know if I can forgive him for going out with another woman while he was married. My mom told him to get out and now he's going to that other woman's house and he will play with her kids! That's the part that really makes me furious!

While we're waiting for my dad to get all his

things out of the house we are staying at my aunt's. I'm trying to have a good summer but the way things are happening it's pretty hard.
P.S. I really do love my dad deep down inside.

Alana, age 11

All those mixed-up feelings!

Of course kids are going to blame the parent who wants the divorce, especially if that parent has fallen in love with someone else.

In a movie called *Shoot the Moon* there is an emotional scene in which a twelve-year-old girl runs away from her mother's house and hides outside the house where her father is now living with another woman. As the girl looks through the living room window she sees her father playing hearts with this woman's little boy and it hurts her very much. After all, he is *her* father. He used to play hearts with her.

Dear Judy,

I'm miserable. I don't know what to do. I don't like the guy my mom is going to marry. She doesn't care about me anymore. I get to see my dad about every two weeks. What should I do? I need your help.

Darlene, age 11

Dear Judy,

I know that you don't know me but my name is Stacy. I just found out that my dad is getting married to a girl I've never met. My parents got a divorce last March. I am writing you because I needed to talk to someone. I am feeling terrible. I should talk it over with my mom but I can't.

Stacy, age 12

Dear Judy,
  My friend Cassie's parents got a divorce. Cassie's dad got both kids. He also got married again. Cassie cries a lot and doesn't think very highly of herself. Could this be because of the divorce?
  Cassie doesn't like her stepmother much. But she loves her real mom very, very much. She is always saying how nice her real mom is. How could I help Cassie?

Jane, age 12

Dear Judy,
  I sort of have a communication problem with Mom. I can't put my feelings about my parents' divorce, my uncertainties about the man she married afterwards, and my misgivings about not seeing or hearing from my father for four years into words. Sure, I know kids get over divorce, but for me there will always be that empty remembrance.

Marisa, age 14

Dear Judy,
  I am in fourth grade, almost ten. I have twin brothers who are seven. My mom and dad are divorced. That was the hardest time in my life. Now I have a stepsister and brother. I get con-

fused because my dad tells me one side that's different from my mom's side.

Joy, age 9

Dear Judy,

Hello, my name is Elizabeth. I am going into eighth grade. I have one brother, who is two years older than me. About four years ago my parents got a divorce. Six months after the divorce my mom got remarried. I don't like my stepfather very well. One year after the divorce my dad bought a house in the neighborhood and a girl named Phyllis moved in with him. She has been married twice and has two children who live with her.

My mom doesn't like me to go over to my dad's house because she says it is a bad influence on me because my dad and Phyllis are not married. I love my mom sincerely and don't want to do anything she doesn't want me to do but I love my dad too much to stay away. I have cut back because of Phyllis since I don't like her that much. My dad is supposed to marry her this summer. She asked me to be in the wedding. I said, "No . . . I'm not even coming to the wedding!" I think when I said that it broke my dad's heart.

I don't know if I should go to the wedding and be in their ceremony for my father, or not go because of Phyllis. I'm confused. Help!

Elizabeth, age 13

Sometimes, kids want to cause their parents pain to pay them back for the pain *they* caused during the divorce. In one family, Kathy, the fourteen-year-old daughter, an only child, destroyed the relationship between her mother and the man she was going to marry. Two years later, during a difficult time in her life, the mother turned to Kathy and shouted, "I could have been happy now if it hadn't been for you!" Kathy shouted back, "Why didn't you tell me off then? Why did you let me get away with ruining it for you?" Kids don't want that kind of power over their parents. It's too frightening. And they don't want to feel responsible for their parents' happiness either. Nor should they.

Many of the problems of remarriage have to do with expectations. When I remarried so quickly I wanted my kids to like, accept, respect, even love, my new husband. That wasn't realistic. I would say, "Isn't he wonderful?" And my kids would just look at me as if I were crazy. They didn't dislike him. But they didn't think he was so great either.

I also wanted him to love them, to see all of their positive and endearing characteristics. But he didn't. In fact, he had his own ideas about raising children, and they were very different from mine. Too bad we didn't take the time to discover this before we married!

So, in addition to all of our other problems, we had an extremely tense situation in which *I* felt caught in the middle, between loyalty to my children and the desire to make this new marriage work. He admitted that he felt jealous of the time and attention I gave to my children. He didn't want to share me with them or with anyone else. Life became an impossible competition.

Kids: When one parent remarries you may feel that your other parent, whom you also love very much, is being replaced. Also, the parent who is remarrying will expect you to share in his or her happiness. But you may feel disloyal to one parent if you allow yourself to be happy for the other. You may feel caught in the middle again! Some kids will try to do everything they can to destroy their parent's new marriage or love affair and then feel guilty. Even though your feelings are normal your parents shouldn't allow you to control their personal lives. That would be destructive for everyone. Adjustments take time. Don't keep your feelings to yourself. If you can't talk about them with your parents at least write them down in a journal or diary. If you can't get rid of your bad feelings ask for help! Remember, none of it is your fault.

Dear Judy,

I've got this problem that I've got to talk to you about. Well, to start with, today my mom's boyfriend jumped all over me because I didn't help feed the horses. I thought *he* was going to feed them because he usually does. So then he said, "Well, if you can't help you can just forget about riding!" So you see, my mom's boyfriend is my problem.

Mom keeps saying she is going to leave him but she never does. Before he came I used to be able to talk to mom and tell her my feelings. But I can't now because everything I tell her she tells him. And I don't trust him.

Brenda, age 10

Trust, like friendship and respect, goes both ways and has to be earned. Both take time to develop. If the new person in your life doesn't treat your kids with respect, for whatever reason, you better let him or her know it right away, before those negative feelings and behavior patterns grow and become even more destructive. Try to talk about it without becoming defensive.

I know that can be hard to do. I was so defensive about my children following my divorce that a critical word could send me into a frenzy. Much of that was my own divorce guilt. On the other hand, we can be so afraid of jeopardizing our new love relationships that we sometimes forget our children's needs.

Dear Judy,

My name is Connie. I am thirteen years old and going into eighth grade. Three years ago my parents went through a divorce and we had a lot of problems. Since then I have lived with my mom two times and my dad one time but now I'm going back with my dad again. Sometimes I get along with my stepfather and sometimes I don't. He has a drinking problem, but he is trying to quit. He's not doing too good of a job. The past three years have been real bad for me.

I was an honor student and always got good grades until there was all of that family trouble. Last summer my mother almost had a nervous breakdown because I went to Colorado for the summer to stay with my aunt and uncle. I didn't want to come back and that hurt my mom inside. I love my mom a lot but sometimes (very often) we just don't get along. My father and I get along very well.

Connie, age 13

Dear Judy,

I'm writing because I was just crying and I need someone to talk to. You see, my problem is: my mom got divorced when I was nine years old (I'm twelve now) and she just got married three months ago. Now she's pregnant. I'm not worried about having a little brother or sister. The problem is my stepfather.

I'm almost positive he doesn't like me because he thinks I never do any work. My mom came in my room one evening before dinner and told me that I'd better start doing some work around here to make my stepfather happy. She said he told her I never do any work (wash the dishes, clean my room, etc.). I immediately began to cry and I told her I worked my butt off around this house. I could barely keep from crying during dinner.

I love my mom but sometimes I hate her, too. I also love my real dad more than anyone in the world, except God. I really hate my mother for divorcing my dad. Whenever she talks about him now she'll say, "Your father called." I hate it when mom says *your father*. I know that dad was her husband and now he's not. I think she wants to start a whole new life. I'll bet she wouldn't admit that she was married to the most wonderful man in the world.

Kerry, age 12

All kids hate it when one divorced parent refers to the other as *your mother* or *your father*. If it's too hard to refer to your ex as *Mom* or *Dad* when you're talking to your kids, then it's better to use first names. First names have less hostility. I have heard this complaint many times, starting with my own children, who hated it when John referred to me as *your mother*.

Kids feel more comfortable calling their stepparents by their first names, too. I don't know why adults should resent this. It only makes kids more hostile to be forced into calling a stranger *Mom* or *Dad*. It has nothing to do with respect.

Dear Judy,

I am a twelve-year-old girl and an only child. My mom and dad first separated when I was only four. Now both of them are remarried. My mom and stepfather live in Boston and I live with my dad and stepmother in Hartford.

My stepmother, Wendy, was only fourteen when I was born so she isn't old enough to be my mother. She sometimes treats me younger than I am and doesn't realize that kids make mistakes, too. I feel sorry for her being that way, even though it hurts me. She doesn't always let me wear the clothes I like and have my hair the way I want it.

Sharon, age 12

When I wrote back to Sharon I suggested that because she writes so well and is able to put her feelings into words she should write a letter to Wendy, telling her exactly how she feels and why. I told her she should be kind, so that Wendy's feelings wouldn't be hurt, but that she should also be honest. And I encouraged her to try to talk to Wendy after Wendy read the letter.

It's very hard, in the beginning, to live in a stepfamily situation. I know, because I'm a stepmother, too, and it's the hardest role I've ever played.

It might help if Wendy read some books about kids, to bring back her own childhood memories and feelings and put her in touch with Sharon's. Probably, because Wendy is so young, she feels a great responsibility in being a stepparent. I asked Sharon if she had talked with her father about the situation. And I told her if she couldn't find a way to bring up the subject herself, to share my letter with him, for a start.

Dear Judy,

I saw you on a TV show a couple of weeks ago. You said, "It's terrible, but I have never received a positive letter from one of my young readers concerning a stepmother." Oh, God! The hopelessness of that statement overwhelmed me and had me sobbing and depressed.

I am a thirty-year-old stepmother of three. The middle child, a sixteen-year-old girl, has lived with us for two years. I suppose I'm fortunate that she really doesn't seem to hate me but, rather, considers me a nuisance. Most of the time I simply don't exist to her. For two years this girl has been the center of my concern and attention and she, basically, doesn't talk to me. Often, she doesn't even look at me. *Anguish* sounds so dramatic but it describes my feelings perfectly.

Barbara, adult

It's hard to like—never mind love—someone who doesn't like you back, who won't look directly at you or even talk to you when the primary parent isn't around. I know how impossible it is when the resentment and the tension at home grow so thick you have to leave in order to relax. I know because I've been there. I know why Barbara calls it anguish. And my only suggestion is to try to look at it from both points of view. Suppose you're a kid and your parent falls in love with someone new. Suddenly you're competing for your parent's attention and affection with a stranger. How do you feel? How do you behave? And doesn't this new person resent you, too? I think what often happens is that, as stepparents, we are so often lacking in confidence that we overreact to every little thing, causing unnecessary resentment.

Sally, a twelve-year-old, used to play one parent against the other. When she was with her father and stepmother, and they did or said something she didn't like, she would call her mother and say she wanted to go home. When she was with her mother and stepfather, if she didn't get her own way, she would threaten to move in with her father. Once her parents realized what was going on and agreed that this wasn't acceptable behavior, nor was it in Sally's best interest, Sally learned to adjust. When she did her relationship with both sets of parents slowly improved.

A panel of four young people, all stepchildren, met at a monthly meeting of the Stepfamily Association of America in New York City (*New York Times*, January 13, 1985). They said that "for fear of jeopardizing relations with the new spouse, the parent would often not speak up for them and seemed wary of asking for time alone with them.

"'Sometimes I would just like to go to the movies with my dad,' one boy said, 'but my dad is afraid of leaving his new wife home alone.' One girl pointed out that she would sometimes leave dirty dishes in the sink, just like any other teenager, but that her stepmother repeatedly accused her of doing it just to hurt her. 'She was unable to see that it was just because I was lazy,' the girl said, 'that it didn't have anything to do with her.'

"How long does it take to get used to a new stepparent? At least two years, maybe longer. 'You don't just wake up the next morning and love one another.'" You don't even wake up the next morning necessarily liking one another. But don't give up!

3

When One Parent Dies and the Other Remarries

Dear Judy,

My mom died two years ago and last year my dad got remarried and it's the pits. My stepmother doesn't like any of my friends, doesn't like my boyfriend, she even made me change schools. Just the other night after drill team practice I came home and asked my dad if I could play soccer for Mapleton Pee Wee teams and he said yes. But then she said no. And all because she said no I don't get to play. Every time I try to tell my dad what's going on he doesn't listen.

Audra, age 12

Dear Judy,

My real dad died when I was in first grade. I am now in sixth grade. I miss my dad. My stepdad is mean to me.

Amy, age 11

A letter from Amy's mother arrived in the same envelope.

Dear Judy,

Amy thinks her stepfather is mean to her because he makes her mind, which she hates to do. Of course, I have spoiled her because of her losing her dad. She has always had her own way and it is my fault but I feel so sorry for her and still do. She loves her stepfather. I know she does.

Amy's mom

Dear Judy,

What I need is advice on my stepmother. I can't get along with her. The problem mostly is because she doesn't like my relatives and she thinks they're "bad people." So, I haven't been calling them for a while. I baby-sit but she does not believe me. She thinks everything I say is a lie and she doesn't trust me or even have confidence in me.

I really hate it when she gives *her* children a pat on the back or a compliment or a kiss. She never does these things to me. When my real mom was alive she gave me these things and many more. My brother and my sister (that is, my real, blood brother and sister) are treated the same way.

Kelly, age 13

Sad to say, the myth of Cinderella is still alive and well. Maybe the clue to all of these stepparent-stepchild relationships is insecurity. Stepparents who feel threatened by the bond between the primary parent and the child can become overly defensive, hostile, domineering, to prove that they have some authority, to prove that they are in control.

I don't know any stepmothers who are part of the primary parental team (that is, who live with their stepchildren most of the time) who haven't had a hard time. All feel like failures. I hear this much more from stepmothers than stepfathers.

Kids whose parents remarry following the death of the other parent are in a different kind of stepfamily situation from those whose parents have divorced and remarried. It's especially important in such a stepfamily for the stepparent not to try to replace the parent who has died. Even though a new spouse may not want to be reminded of how great the deceased husband/wife— mother/father was, the kids have a right to talk about the parent who has died. They need to keep their memories alive. They may want to have photos of that parent around the house. They may want to reminisce. It would be good if the new stepparent didn't turn such feelings into a competition.

Marla, a woman who wrote to me, was divorced with a son and daughter in college when she met and married Len, a widower with two young children. From the beginning there was trouble between Marla and Stacy, her stepdaughter. Seven years later the relationship is still troubled. Stacy complains bitterly about Marla. Marla complains nonstop about Stacy. Len feels caught in the middle.

I wonder, after reading some of these letters, if newly remarried men or women with children are so anxious for life to be serene that they will avoid confrontations at all cost? None of us hears what we don't want to hear. I am reminded again of Randy, telling someone outside the family, "My mother just wants to hear that everything is wonderful."

Another stepmother I know has announced to her family, "There will be no more complaining in this house! I won't listen." Who can blame her? It's no fun living with constant complaints, especially when they're about you. On the other hand, kids can have really important feelings and thoughts to discuss. And someone should be there to listen. That is the job of the primary parent.

Dear Judy,

My name is Dawn. My hobbies are stamp collecting, coin collecting and collecting stuffed animals. I have forty-two of them. My dream is to become a ballerina. I have two brothers. I have a dad. My mom died when I was in third grade. Now I'm in sixth grade. My mom had cancer. My brothers are very, very mean to my father's girlfriend. They make her cry every day.

Dawn, age 12

Dear Judy,

Here's an idea for a book. A thirteen-year-old girl lives in the woods, in Vermont, with her mother and her mother's boyfriend who are hippies. The girl's father committed suicide a year ago. The girl hates to be seen with her mother and un-stepfather. She also lives with the guy's kids (a boy, two years younger and a girl, six). She likes a boy at school but can't get him to be more than a good friend. What a mess!

Geri, age 13

Kids have very little to say about what happens to them. Geri's mother made a decision and Geri is stuck with it. Maybe it will work out, maybe not, but Geri has to cope.

And adults have to cope with the feelings and behavior of their children, and that can hurt terribly, too. I remember crying over my children's attitude toward me and my new love. It's my life, too, I told myself. Don't I have the right to be happy?

Yes, sure . . . but kids think in terms of their own lives, not their parents', of their own happiness and well-being, not their parents'. Parents, on the other hand, have to consider not only their own feelings and needs but those of their kids. And it can be especially hard when you're trying to get your life together after such a loss. But that's a responsibility of parenthood.

4

Confronting Your Parents' Sexuality

Dear Judy,

I'm eleven. I would like to know about your kids, I mean, how they like having you as a mother. I know you are divorced. So are my parents. Well, they're not really. Actually, they weren't married when they had me. I used to hate my father. But he writes me and sends postcards of where he's been. He also writes to my mom. But now I have a stepfather. I dislike him, too. When I heard that he and my mom made love I almost croaked! Wow . . . was that a surprise! But I got over it within a month or so.

Annabelle, age 11

Dear Judy,

I'm ten and I know all there is to know about sex. My parents are divorced but they both got remarried to different people. I have a baby sister who is eight months old. My parents got divorced three years ago. My stepfather was living with us before he and my mother got married so is it possible that they could have done it before the wedding?

Whitney, age 10

Dear Judy,

My parents have been divorced since I was just two years old. I live with my mom. Two years after the divorce she started seeing this man, Michael. They were obviously in love. But I was too young to understand anything about it. Michael came to live with us. I really liked him but I kept wondering why *he* could live with mom and my daddy couldn't.

My main reason for writing to you is because maybe you could write something to help me get over this yucky feeling of first of all thinking that only young people "live" together without being married (not forty- and sixty-year-old people and especially not your own mother!).

I feel weird going into their room in the morning and finding my mother in bed with someone who she's not even married to. And I feel yucky knowing that he has his pants off too.

Regina, age 12

Kids don't want to think about their parents' sexuality. But after a divorce, when one or both parents fall in love again, it's hard to avoid. It can be especially hard for young teens, who are just beginning to deal with their own sexuality. Sometimes the child acts out. "I'm just doing what you're doing, Mother!" my friend's fifteen-year-old daughter shouted, when her mother told her she was staying out too late at night.

When Carole, who had been divorced for five years, found herself in love again, she and Steve decided to live together. But as soon as Steve moved into Carole's house her teenaged kids reported to their father that Carole didn't care about them anymore. "She's only interested in sex with her new boyfriend," they said. What may be right for the parent is not necessarily what the kids see as right for themselves.

A few years ago, at a monthly meeting of Parents Without Partners, I led a discussion on "Sleepover Dates and Single Parents." One mother of three teenagers said that she would never tell her children she was spending the night with a man. Instead, she would phone them to say that she had a flat tire and would not be able to get home until morning. I asked her if she thought her children really believed that story. She was quiet for a moment, then laughed and said, "Of course not! But I could never actually admit to such a thing. I wasn't raised that way."

A young girl at the same meeting said that it was okay with her if her mother had boyfriends spend the night. But she didn't want it to be a surprise. She didn't want to wake up in the morning and find someone there. She wanted her mother to tell her in advance so that she wouldn't feel embarrassed.

If you're a single parent who isn't ready to settle into one serious relationship, you don't have to introduce your kids to every date. It can be too confusing. And it can stimulate sexual competition between parent and teen. But when you do fall in love again and either marry or move in together, remember . . . the kids won't be used to having a lovey-dovey couple around the house and may find any display of affection between you and your new love threatening or embarrassing or disgusting.

Mary Ann, at fourteen, heard frightening sounds coming from her mother's bedroom. She thought her mother's boyfriend, who had just moved in, was trying to kill her mother. She awakened her younger sister and together they approached their mother's closed bedroom door. After a few more minutes Mary Ann realized that her mother and her mother's boyfriend were making love. Mary Ann was angry at her mother for having caused her to worry needlessly and she was very uncomfortable with the truth. But she didn't tell her mother how she had felt that morning until three years later.

So, be aware of your kids' feelings. That doesn't mean you can't show affection for each other in front of the kids. Just keep the heavy stuff private.

Kids: Okay . . . so you wish they wouldn't, especially in front of you. After all, they're not teenagers. But give them a break! They're in love.

5

More Than One Divorce?

Dear Judy,

I love your books! I can really relate to them.
My mom has been divorced twice and she is only
twenty-nine. I have a little brother. I'm interested
in sex. I am ten.

Sybil, age 10

Dear Judy,

My brother and I have a big problem. Our
parents are getting a divorce. This is our mother's fourth marriage. Since her second marriage we were thinking about moving in with our
first (real) father. It takes so long to get
used to new relatives. Our new relatives always
yell at us. We feel unwanted. We tried to
run away but our stepsisters squealed on us.
What should we do? How do we cope with
new fathers? Should we go with our real father

or should we stay with our mother or our step-relatives?

Courtney, age 11

Multiple marriages can certainly be confusing to the children. Kids need security. They need to know where they belong. They need to be told that no matter what happens they can depend on their parent or parents.

Divorcing once is hard enough. After sixteen years of marriage it was traumatic for me. But divorcing a second time was even more difficult. After three-and-a-half very painful years my second husband and I finally divorced. We had made a terrible mistake. It's very hard to forgive yourself after such a mistake. I stayed in that marriage much longer than I should have because I was so concerned about how those closest to me would react.

Recently I had a letter from a nine-year-old girl telling me that her parents were divorcing and she felt as if she was in a deep, dark forest and she could not find her way out. She was very frightened. During the years of my second marriage that's exactly how I felt. I was in a deep, dark forest, too, and could not find my way out. I used to tell myself that I would stay married until both my children went off to college. That way it would be easier for them. But in the meantime, two basically decent human beings, who were all wrong for each other, were tearing each other to pieces. I don't think we could have survived two more years together. Finally, I made the decision to take control of my own life. And once that decision was made I began to find my way out of the forest.

I learned from my mistake. I learned that you must mourn the end of one relationship before beginning another. I learned that you can't expect another person to change your life. You have to make those changes yourself. I learned that there are worse things in life than living without a spouse.

I wasn't sure then that I would even take another chance on love. I knew how complicated it could be and I wasn't sure it was worth it.

6

Can It Work?

Dear Judy,

I am eleven years old and I love to read. My mom and dad were divorced when I was only eight months old. My dad was mean to my mom but in a different way, such as making her hate her own mother.

Finally, the divorce came through and my mom got me. We were alone until I was seven, then my mom got together with this guy named Steve. He lived with us on and off for two years and then they got married at the justice of the peace. I was a witness and it was really hard on me. Now, this is our fifth year together and he is really terrific once I gave him a chance!

Holly, age 11

Dear Judy,

I am almost ten and my parents are divorced. I live with my mother and stepfather. My real father smokes joints. Will you write a book about a girl who doesn't want to be with her real father in the summer and wants to be with her stepfather instead? Please do. I also want my stepfather's last name.

Peggy, age 10

Dear Judy,
    My parents have been divorced since I was six. I live with my mother and stepfather. My father lives in California and we live in New York. I love my father very, very much. I see him as often as I can. I also like my stepfather. He doesn't have any other children. He wasn't married before like most stepfathers so I am important to him. I know because I once asked him if he wanted to have kids of his own and he said that having me is enough.

Madeline, age 12

Of course I took another chance on love, complications and all. And this time it works. We get along really well. We laugh at the same jokes. We genuinely like each other. We respect each other. And probably, we're a lot more mellow now than we were when we were younger. That helps us cope with the stress of stepfamily life.
    George's daughter, Amanda, has been an important part of my life since she was twelve. She has lived with us for several months each year, both during the school term and in the summer. She and I have had our ups

and downs. In the beginning she thought, Wow . . . Judy Blume . . . wait till I tell my friends who my father is living with! I think she was disappointed when she found out that I am just an ordinary person and that life with me wouldn't be perfect.

The most difficult years were Amanda's fourteenth and fifteenth. A friend, who is a family counselor, helped me through that period. When I cried, "Help! I don't know how to live with a young teenager and not be a mother," my friend suggested that I pretend that Amanda was a guest. "Pretend she's a friend of your daughter's who has come to spend a month with you. You'd certainly tell her the house rules, such as dirty laundry goes in the basket next to the washing machine, not on the bathroom floor. And you'd expect her to help with meals, by setting the table, or cutting up the salad. But you wouldn't tell her how, when or where to do her schoolwork, and you wouldn't tell her what time to go to bed. She has a primary parent in the house, her father. He will make the rules."

I came rushing into the house that afternoon, calling, "Amanda . . . I think I've got it figured out now."

That didn't solve all our problems, but it certainly helped. And every year we feel more comfortable together. Amanda is a college student now.

When George first came into my life I told Randy, who was away at college, "He's very nice. I think you'll like him." She replied, "Don't tell me who to like, Mother. I'll make up my own mind." And in time, she did. Over the years a genuine friendship has developed between my children and George. Of course, Randy and Larry don't live with us. They were pretty much on their own when we met. But when we're together, it works. Maybe because I'm less defensive this time. I don't feel caught in the middle. Maybe because George and I can laugh at ourselves and even at our children. Neither one of us thinks our children are perfect. And we certainly know that we aren't.

I can't say whether what my children feel for either of their stepparents is love. But that doesn't matter. I know they're glad that John and I are both happy. And they certainly feel an affection for both stepparents.

If you are in a stepfamily and there are problems (and there are bound to be problems) yell for help! We come to stepfamily life with no preparation, with no experience. We don't know how to do it and then we are ashamed and guilty when it doesn't work. From time to time every one of us resents the intrusion of the other's children. But we don't want to let those feelings fester and lead to even more problems. Maybe before we merge our families we should be required to complete a course. I wish I had known about the Stepfamily Association of America, whose monthly meetings and bulletin would have helped me very much. Their address is listed in the Resources section at the back of the book.

Try to keep your expectations realistic. Try to remember that love is not a competition, and that help is available. If there is trouble, don't wait. You aren't the first stepfamily to have problems and you won't be the last. With the current divorce rate we better figure out how to make stepfamilies work. Because when you get right down to it, most of us do want to share our lives. Most of us do try again.

Chapter V
WHEN SOMEONE YOU LOVE DIES

Dear Judy,

My name is Hillary. My mother died Friday and I went to her funeral today. I am ten and a half and my little brother is six. I wish you would write a book about the feelings of a person when someone like a parent dies. My feelings are that I am left here with nobody like a mom to understand a growing girl's problems. I am alone except for my dad and brother. I wish you would write back with some hope to get me back on the track. Please!

Hillary, age 10

I know how hard it is to lose someone you love. My father died suddenly, when I was twenty-one. He died at home on a sunny Sunday afternoon in July. We had just returned from the airport, where we had met my brother and sister-in-law, who had been stationed overseas for four years. David and his wife were expecting their first child. And I was to be married in a few weeks. As my father was driving home from the airport, he said, "What a banner year for our family!"

My father was fifty-four years old and full of plans for my wedding. He hoped that when I came down the aisle on his arm I would raise my veil and kiss him goodbye. In his workshop was the chest of drawers he was building for the studio apartment where John and I would live after we were married.

My father had never been sick but when we returned from the airport he said he felt strange and he lay down on the sofa. I knew something was terribly wrong. "What lousy timing," he whispered to me as I sat on the floor holding his hand, waiting for the doctors to arrive. But there was nothing they could do. Within an hour of the time we got home from the airport my father was dead of a coronary thrombosis.

He had been the youngest of seven children. Two of his brothers had been dentists, like he was. Both of them had died in their early forties. One of them left three sons. I worried when I was nine and ten, that my father would die, too. I made bargains with God. I became ritualistic, inventing prayers that had to be repeated seven times a day, in order to keep my father safe and healthy. I felt responsible for his well-being—a terrible burden for a child. I couldn't share my fears about my father's death. I believed that if I told anyone about them they would really come true.

I wrote about a child's fear of the death of a parent in *Starring Sally J. Freedman as Herself*. And I wrote about the sudden, violent death of a parent in *Tiger Eyes*. A few years ago when I was a guest on the TV show, *Late Night America*, the host, Dennis Wholey, asked me what was the single most significant experience of my childhood. I answered spontaneously,

"Death." By the time I was twenty-one and my father died, I had already experienced the deaths of three grandparents, seven aunts and uncles and a twenty-five-year-old cousin. I had grown up sitting shivah, the Jewish tradition of a week of mourning following the death of a loved one. And yet, thanks to my father, there was so much joy in our house! There were family picnics and celebrations, there were parties and games and jokes and laughter. My father believed in making every day count.

Dear Judy,

I am eleven years old. I would like to write a book about myself. I think I'm very different from other kids and I don't have very many friends. I talk to the wind and I tell my house goodnight. I've never told anybody that, not even my mother. I would like to express my troubles and my worries and my happy thoughts and times without letting people know it's me in the book.

My father died a year ago and I'm still feeling pretty low so I thought writing a book about my bad feelings would maybe make me feel better about my father and other very depressing problems. Maybe more people will like me.

I thought you would be the best person plus the one I would be most comfortable talking to about this. Please answer soon.

Edie, age 11

Dear Judy,

I am ten years old. My father died in January. He was not shot, like Davey's father in *Tiger*

Eyes. He had a heart attack. He was a drunk and I was very sad because I wished he would go away, but not die. Every time I think about it I break down in tears because we weren't close.

Another thing is, after my father died, my mother started going out with someone. That reminds me of Davey's mother going out with the Nerd.

Michelle, age 10

Dear Judy,

My name is Ashley. I'm fifteen years old. When I was younger, my father was killed flying a helicopter for the police. It took me a long time before I was able to talk about my father without crying. I am seeing a counselor right now who is trying to help a group of us with family problems.

I know how Davey, in the book *Tiger Eyes,* felt when her mother started seeing that man you called the Nerd because my mom was recently married to a man. I try to like him but it's hard. I sometimes feel he might try to take the place of my father and no one could ever do that.

Your book has helped me understand my feelings and to know I have to be strong, if only for my mother's sake. I have gotten my mom to read it, too, and hope it helps her as much as it did me.

Ashley, age 15

Dear Judy,

Hi! My name is Simone. I'm fourteen. In September I will go to high school. But I feel scared. I don't know how to tell you my feelings.

My dad died last year soon after we came to America. He got cancer. I got so sad. Still, I didn't tell my friends that he died. I just didn't want to. But sometimes they ask about my parents like, "Are your parents split?" or questions like that. I don't know what to tell them.

Simone, age 14

I couldn't talk about my father's death to my mother. It's been twenty-five years and I still can't. But I was able to talk to other people and even now I can reminisce about him with some of my old friends. No matter what your age it's important to be able to talk about your feelings and about the person you love who has died. Talking about it helps you accept it and it helps to keep your memories alive.

Dear Judy,

I just finished reading *Tiger Eyes*. My teacher suggested it for me because I lost my dad in September. My dad died on the couch. I found him there. He had a heart attack. It was really scary because I was so close to him. He was trying to get me on a gymnastics team. I haven't got there yet. We moved to an apartment building recently. My mom still cries at night. It doesn't feel the same doing things without my dad. I miss him but life goes on.

Emily, age 15

When I was very young it was my father who made life seem exciting. Whether I was sitting on his workbench, hammering nails into a piece of wood, or painting the outside of my playhouse beside him, I felt safe and secure. He cut my toenails, he took my temperature when I was sick, he taught me to print my name. I don't know what my life would have been like if he had died when I was younger. It is always hard to lose a parent, but to lose your parent before you have the chance to know him or her as an adult, is especially hard. My father knew that I loved him and I knew that he loved me, and so, I am able to think of him happily.

After each funeral in our family my father would remind us that "life goes on . . ." but because he died just weeks before I was married, the first year of my marriage was very difficult. I felt so guilty. How could I be happy when my mother was so unhappy? How could I be starting a new life when the life she knew had ended? I knew that my father wouldn't have wanted me to feel guilty. I knew he would have reminded me that "life goes on . . ." and it does.

Dear Judy,

I know you aren't any psychiatrist or Abby, but I thought you would be able to help me with my problem since you seem to be like us. Anyways, recently my grandfather died. He was so wonderful. It seems impossible for him to be gone. I keep thinking he is on some long trip and will return soon. And that's not even half my problem. It seems as if everyone is changing now. My mom and dad and aunts and uncles seem to be having a need for the inheritance money. I don't know what to do.

Doria, age 11

Dear Judy,

My name is Victoria. I am almost eleven. I have two younger brothers. My grandfather died last year. I was so angry at him for dying and then when the anger was gone I was so sad. My brothers were always crying and my little cousin, who was only four, didn't even realize what had happened.

The night my grandfather died my uncle called. My father answered the phone and in a few seconds he started to choke. I ran to get him a glass of water and when I came back to the room my mother was crying. She cried harder and harder. Then Daddy said, "Grandpa's dead." I stood motionless. I couldn't say anything. Then I burst out in tears.

That night I couldn't sleep. I heard my brothers snoring lightly. I lay awake staring at the ceiling. I couldn't figure out why he had to die. It just wasn't fair. I didn't understand.

We went to stay with my grandmother for a while and I kept thinking that I saw my grandfather. I was so scared I couldn't stand it. Then my friend came to visit and made me feel much better. She was there when I needed her. When it was time to go home again I hated to leave my grandma but she said she would be fine.

We've all come a long way since then. I'm not afraid anymore. And I'm glad that I can accept his death now.

Victoria, age 11

Dear Judy,

My grandmother died two years ago. She had a stroke. For a few months I felt numb and I didn't cry. Then one night I was talking to a friend about grandparents and I just started to cry. After I did I felt a lot better. Now I can talk about my grandmother and I don't feel sad. I feel the love I have for her.

Susan, age 11

My grandmother (my mother's mother) was sick for a long time before she died from cancer. We had been very close. She lived with us for the two school years we spent in Florida and even after our return to New Jersey, she spent a lot of time at our house, although she made her home with my aunt and uncle. Because they both worked, she moved in with us when she became ill, so my mother could care for her.

No one really talked to me about her illness. I was a young teenager and I knew it was serious. I knew it was cancer. But I didn't know or understand any of the details. My grandmother went to the hospital for the last time a few weeks before I went away to summer camp. I visited her the day before I left but I didn't really know what to say or how to act. My mother said that Nanny was happy just to see me.

My parents called me at camp a month later, to tell me that my grandmother had died. The call came during dinner. When I heard the news I couldn't speak, I couldn't respond at all. I felt this gigantic lump in my throat and I hung up the phone before my parents were finished talking to me. They called right back to see if I was all right. I managed to say that I was. Then I returned to the dining hall and took my place at the table. But I couldn't eat. Rachel, my friend from home, asked me what was wrong. I whispered that my grandmother had died. Then I stood up and ran out of the dining hall. Rachel followed me. Although we hadn't been close that summer she knew my grandmother and she understood what I was feeling.

I didn't attend the evening activity. I sat outside under a tree, by myself, looking at the stars. After a while a counselor came and sat with me. He talked to me about death, about losing someone you love. He encouraged me to talk to him. But I wasn't ready to talk about my grandmother or to share what I was feeling.

I didn't go home for my grandmother's funeral. My parents thought it would be better for me to stay at camp. I think my parents thought my grandmother's funeral would be too emotional an experience for me. They were trying to protect me.

Now I believe it would have been better if I had gone to her funeral. I was fifteen and my grandmother had been an important part of my life. I should have been there to say goodbye, and to share the sorrow of my family.

Dear Judy,
    Recently a little boy, seven years old, was killed. He was very close to me and I miss him a lot.

Helene, age 15

Dear Judy,
    My name is Maria. I'm in the sixth grade, going into seventh. One of my friends went into the hospital because of heart problems. He almost died on the operating table but they brought him back to life. Then, in the recovery room, one of

the tubes in his chest popped out and he lost air from his heart and his brain. He went into a coma. Then he died.

It's hard to talk about this incident because I liked my friend very much. He was a good friend to me. Almost every day he would ask me for a pencil. I've been thinking of writing a letter about what I felt. It's like there's an empty space in my heart. I think it's for him.

Maria, age 12

Losing a friend, no matter what your age, is another kind of loss. It forces you to face your own mortality in a way that the death of a parent or grandparent does not. My friend, Lee, died two summers ago. She had been sick for a long time and we knew that she wouldn't get well. I flew to Santa Fe to say goodbye to her. We held hands and talked and cried. She had a wonderful sense of humor and she made me laugh, even then. It's still hard for me to accept Lee's death. When I'm in Santa Fe I expect to see her, and more than once I have picked up the phone to dial her number.

My first experience with the death of a friend came the summer I was nine and a girl in my group at day camp died suddenly. I didn't understand how someone my age could possibly die. What I remember my parents telling me is that Beatrice was at the beach with her family when she felt a terrible pain in her head, and then she collapsed and died. For a long time after that I worried that if I got a headache I might die suddenly, too.

If your children know a child who has died, encourage them to talk about it with you. Try to answer their questions honestly but reassure them at the same time.

If you shy away from the issue they will sense your discomfort and worry even more.

As a parent, I can't think of anything more tragic than losing a child. A few years ago I received a phone call from a frantic father who heard that I was coming to the Detroit area for a convention. He begged me to visit his ten-year-old daughter, who was terminally ill. My editor Dick Jackson and I went to the house and I spent a few minutes alone with Marcy. She told me that when she grew up she wanted to be a writer. She enjoyed writing very much but she couldn't write much anymore because she was so tired. Her father called me a few months later, to tell me that she had died.

When I was young my mother warned me not to love too deeply because the pain of losing someone you love is so great. But I couldn't live my life fearing loss. My father taught me that life should be appreciated and lived to the fullest, that every day is a new experience, that there are ups and downs but I didn't have to dwell on the downs. That's the gift he gave to me. The gift of appreciating life. The thing about loving is, you never have to stop. Even when that person is gone, you can still love and remember and keep him or her in your heart.

Chapter VI
DEAR DIARY

Dear Judy,

From now on you're going to be getting a lot of letters from me. I'm going to tell you everything that's on my mind. Things that I can't tell my parents or my friends. You don't have to answer every letter. I know you've got other things to do. I just like writing to you. It's like talking to a friend.

Kelly, age 13

So many kids write to me because the act of writing down what's on their minds is often enough to help them feel better. That's why, when I write back to them, I suggest that they get a notebook or a diary or journal—it doesn't really matter—and write in it whenever they feel the need. Journal writing might not be for everyone, but for kids who feel comfortable with the idea, and for kids who write easily, it can be a valuable tool—one that lasts a lifetime.

Dear Judy,

Last Christmas a friend gave me a diary. Although I had started to keep diaries before I never really committed myself to them. This diary, though, saved my sanity and perhaps, my life. This diary made me want to write. It helped me through the most difficult year of my life. It lifted me out of a gloominess that nearly ended in suicide. It took away the hurt, added to my few joys, relieved my anger and halted my tears.

As I read back through my diary one statement I see at the bottom of an October page sort of explains what I felt this year. *I'm scared . . . I'm so scared. I wish somebody would talk to me and tell me it's going to be all right.*

This whole year everything I went through I went through all *alone.* I've promised myself that from now on I will find someone to talk to. But a promise to yourself is too easy to break so I am promising you and this will make me think twice before going back on my word.

This is a year I will never forget. I have grown and learned in many ways.

Missy, age 14

I was given a five-year diary when I was in fifth grade. It had a brown leather cover and a tiny lock and key. The dates were printed on each page in gold ink. I thought it was beautiful and I loved the idea of writing in it every day. But I didn't know what I was supposed to write and so, I hardly wrote in it at all. Soon I became discouraged and gave up. I wasn't ready for a diary.

Janice, a mother who wrote to me last year, said that she had given a diary to her daughter, Christine, for her tenth birthday. A week later, when Janice went to Christine's room to kiss her goodnight, she found Christine in tears. "What's wrong?" Janice asked. "I can't think of anything to write in my diary!" Christine sobbed, throwing it across the room. Janice blamed herself for choosing a gift that made Christine feel like a failure. Christine wasn't ready for a diary either.

If you do give your kids a diary tell them that they don't have to write in it every day. That's the whole point. There are no rules. Encourage your kids to write whenever they feel like it and assure them that you will respect their privacy.

I began to keep a diary again when I was in high school. I found it satisfying to confide in my diary, as many teenagers do. But to protect myself, in case—God forbid—my mother ever found it, I invented code words so that she would not know what I was talking about.

Dear Judy,

I have a story to tell you. It is about a black girl who had no one to talk to. She did have a lot of friends but no one that she could really sit down and talk to. Not even her own mother would talk to her, for her mother was far too busy to have a few words with her oldest daughter. She was the oldest of five children. She had a stepfather but he was never home. They all lived in a small apartment.

Because she had no one to talk to she kept

everything to herself. She was very smart but she had a lot on her mind. She would daydream and sometimes act dumb. That was not good. She even got sick a lot!

Someone noticed what was going on and saw that she was an intelligent girl with too much on her mind. So a diary was given to her for Christmas and she liked the idea of having one. It helped her unload a lot that was on her mind. It became the one true friend she had.

But her mother never liked the idea of her having the diary. So months later her mother started to read it and found out a lot of things about her that she didn't like. The girl found out and tried to run away but she had nowhere to go so she went back home. Her mother found out why she ran away and took the diary away. Her mother even tried to use the diary and what the girl had written in it against her.

Now the girl hates everyone and everything. The story goes on to tell what the girl goes through with her family and how she may go crazy.

Francesca, age 16

Toward the end of my seventeenth summer I discovered that my mother had been reading my diary. I knew because, to ensure my privacy, I had devised an intricate way of wrapping rubber bands around it and one day I noticed that they had not been properly replaced.

It was the summer of 1955 and my parents and I were driving from New Jersey to California, to visit relatives. I was bored on the long, hot, dusty drive and wished I had taken a job at a summer camp instead. I missed my friends and I longed for excitement. I was moody, sullen and irritable. I wrote about my hostile feelings in my diary every night.

I was furious at my mother when I found out she had read my diary. (And I was also embarrassed by what I had written. The code words I'd invented covered my love life, which was nonexistent that summer, but not my feelings about traveling with my family.) Still, I didn't confront my mother right away. Instead, I slept with my diary under my pillow every night and didn't let it out of my sight during the day. Months later, when I finally did confront my mother, she confessed that she had read my diary that summer because I had seemed so unhappy. She thought it might give her a clue as to what was wrong. I could not forgive her for reading my diary and I vowed that when I had children I would respect their privacy.

But when Randy was sixteen she seemed to change, almost overnight. I felt as if I didn't know her anymore. One day, when she didn't return from school as expected, and I was worried sick, I went to her room. I found her diary on a shelf in the closet. I sat on her bed for a long time, holding the diary, blaming myself for everything that had gone wrong. In spite of my vow to respect her privacy, I finally opened it and read the last few entries. It was clear that she was feeling alienated, frightened and confused and that we needed help.

When she finally returned, late that night, I told her I had read some of her diary. I still don't know if she was more angry or more relieved. With help we began to work out our problems.

I can't excuse myself for having read Randy's diary. I don't want my kids or anyone else to read my journal. What I write tonight may have nothing to do with how I am feeling tomorrow. I tend to write in my journal when I am troubled, confused, tense or angry. I find that writing about whatever is on my mind relieves the tension and helps me sort out my feelings. Often it is just the mood of the moment. I rarely write about my good times. I'm not interested in keeping a record of my life. Writing in my journal offers me an emotional outlet.

Chapter VII
KIDS REALLY
NEED TO KNOW . . .

1

About Puberty

Dear Judy,
    My mom's scared to tell me anything so could you please write a book called *How to Tell My Daughter* so I can give it to her.

Karen, age 12

I know how Karen feels. I wish my parents had had a book when I was young, to help them answer my questions. I was so desperate for information that when I was in sixth grade I looked up the word *puberty* in the *Webster's* dictionary in our classroom. I knew that that word was connected in some mysterious way to growing up and the idea of growing up was exciting. But what I found in the dictionary didn't help much. "Puberty: the period or age at which a person is first capable of sexual reproduction of offspring." It didn't answer any of my questions. It didn't say anything about my feelings, fears, or my need to feel normal. During that year I was obsessed by the idea of menstruation and breast development and so were all my friends. We talked about it nonstop, but none of us really understood it. At night I would pray, "Please God . . . just let me be normal!"

Dear Judy,

I read in the newspaper that someone said if a person from another planet read *Are You There God? It's Me, Margaret* they would think all girls are preoccupied with their bodies. Well, most of the time we are!

I'm a lot like Margaret in the sense that I worry if I'm normally developed. When I got my period for the first time (last month) I was so surprised! I just got out my copy of *Are You There God? It's Me, Margaret* and it kind of reminded me that I'm not alone. Being eleven can be tough!

Tess, age 11

Dear Judy,

I used to wonder if I was normal when surrounded by other boys. I would always compare my voice, my hair, my size and the rest of me, to them. Then I would worry.

Dennis, age 14

Dear Judy,

I have two daughters, ages eight and eleven, and I've promised myself that I won't make the mistakes my own mother made with me. Because of my sheltered upbringing I still don't know what is normal and what is not and I am forty-one years old.

Martha, adult

Dear Judy,

I am in the fifth grade and developing. It is kind of embarrassing having people say things like, "Lorna stuffs." I don't really "stuff" but once word gets spread around you can't stop it. Many times I have been alerted for my period. I was embarrassed asking my mother if she thought I had it, so I asked my understanding sister what was in my underwear. She looked at it and said that it was just something called "discharge." I really don't know what that is but my sister said it is just a part of growing up.

I have an interest in a boy in my class and he seems to have an interest in me. Hopefully it isn't because I'm growing (like last year). I am already 5'2" and wear a size 9 in women's shoes. I would like to know if you think I am a *normal* fifth grader. Please write back.

Lorna, age 11

Kids want reassurance that they're normal. Every week they write asking if I think they're okay. They ask me to explain what their parents haven't. They wish their parents would talk to them about sex. They wish their parents would answer their questions honestly and to the point. But some parents become nervous as their children approach puberty. Some even get angry when their children begin to ask questions, sending out the message that this is a subject we are never going to discuss. Kids can sense their parents' fear and discomfort, so they go elsewhere for their information. That often means they wind up with misinformation.

A man I know, well-educated and sophisticated in

many ways, once told me that his children would learn about sex on the street, the same way he did, because if it was good enough for him, it's good enough for them. But it isn't good enough and it never was.

Dear Judy,

I am forty-one years old and have one son who is twelve. Times change, but people do not. Anyone can tell me their boy or girl will be told things when they are older. What it boils down to is that parents are telling their children too late. They are telling them what they already know. Yet I still hear, "But my child didn't know about it and was so embarrassed when I told him."

I am sure the child was embarrassed, but only for the parents. How very sad I feel for people who feel that a normal body happening is too shameful to speak about.

Anita, adult

Dear Judy,

My friend's parents are too shy to talk about sex with her. So she doesn't know anything about it. She learns it from the kids at school who don't know half of what they are saying.

Lilly, age 13

Dear Judy,

I'm twelve years old and going into seventh grade. I'm real excited about junior high. I'm a lot more mature than most of my other friends. Once, out at recess, some kids started talking about puberty and periods and things like that. And you know how that is a very important and special part of becoming a woman or man. (I haven't had mine yet.) Anyway, they started joking about it and making fun of everything. Well, after they started joking and stuff, I just left. I just couldn't stand it.

But I know that people tend to laugh out their fears and worries when they don't know about it. I know it shouldn't be an embarrassing topic but it just is for most people, especially around this age when things start changing.

Amanda, age 12

Dear Judy,

My mother decided to finally have the talk with me. But I knew about that subject long before my mother told me about it. When she was telling me she kept asking me if I had ever heard anything about that. I kept saying no, as if I had never heard a word. But you know how it is, everyone picks everything up on the streets. My mother wasn't the first one to tell me. Actually, she was the last.

Monica, age 12

There's a slogan that I really like: If you can talk with your kids about sex, you can talk with your kids about anything! And it really isn't that hard once you get comfortable with the subject yourself. One reason that parents have trouble talking with their kids about sex is that they aren't sure of the facts themselves. It's one thing to know how to do it, it's another to be able to explain it. Today, there are books available for every age group. Books that can teach you the facts and books that can help you explain them to your kids. Don't wait until your child is twelve. Kids are curious and open up to that age. Once they are fourteen or fifteen many of them don't want to discuss sexuality with their parents. Be ready for those first questions. Your kids will trust you if they learn early on that you tell them the truth. Check the Resources section at the back of the book for a list of books and for agencies that offer bibliographies.

Dear Judy,
  I am in fifth grade and would like to suggest an idea to you. Why don't you write a book on a girl who is at the stage of, "I don't want to be a little girl anymore but then again, I do." I'm like that and it's very hard. Like when I went to my friend's house and she was playing some rock music on the stereo, I wanted to feel like an older kid but I still wanted to be my parents' little girl. I don't want to tell anyone about that.

Jill, age 10

Most kids can't wait to grow up. All of their fantasies involve being grown up. But occasionally I hear from kids who are feeling alone and frightened. If they could talk with their parents they might feel better.

Dear Judy,

My name is Daisy and I wrote to tell you about something I am worrying about. I don't want to grow up. I'm twelve and I still enjoy playing dolls. I always carry my Raggedy Ann with me on trips and when I spend the night with people.

Daisy, age 12

Dear Judy,

I have a lot in common with Margaret, in your book. We both talk to God and I am in a club like hers. But Margaret and I are not alike in one respect. She wants to grow up. I don't. I don't know why I feel this way about growing up. I just do. Maybe my only reason is I'm afraid if I grow up my parents will get old and die. Should I feel this way? Did you ever feel abnormal like I do? I hope I'm not the only one who feels this way about life but I feel so alone in the world. I hope you can help me.

Kristen, age 11

Growing up doesn't happen overnight, although I used to think it did. I used to think that as soon as I developed breasts and my periods began I would be grown up. Then I thought, When I am fifteen I will really be grown up. And then I thought, When I graduate from high school and go off to college I will definitely be grown up. After that it was getting married and having babies. Then, finding work. At forty, I finally figured out that growing up is a continuing process.

Dear Judy,

I don't really know too much about growing up. I guess it's because I haven't finished doing it yet.

Angela, age 10

2

About Menstruation

Dear Judy,
  I don't understand about when you start your period or when you start growing everything. I'm ten and a half, almost eleven. I think I have everything but I'm not sure. When did you find out?

Mary, age 10

When I was about nine we went to visit my aunt and uncle on Long Island. My cousin, Grace, wasn't feeling well that day and when I asked her what was wrong she said, "You'll find out when you're thirteen."

On the long drive home to New Jersey I asked my parents over and over again *what* I would find out when I was thirteen. They kept changing the subject. Finally, before I went to sleep that night, I asked my father one more time, "What will I find out when I'm thirteen?"

He took me on his lap and tried to explain menstruation to me. But it was a very confusing explanation. There was something about eggs dropping down, something about blood and something about a lunar cycle, leading me to believe that every time the moon was full every female in the world over the age of thirteen was menstruating. It didn't make a lot of sense to me.

A year later I was in a public women's room with my mother and she bought a pad from the machine on the wall. "Do you know what this is for?" she asked.

"Yes," I answered, embarrassed.

"Someday it will happen to you," she said.

"I know," I said. But I still didn't understand exactly what would happen or why.

That was the last time either one of my parents ever talked to me about menstruation. No one gave me a book and no one discussed what I should do if I got my first period away from home.

Dear Judy,

I just got my period a couple of months ago and my mom hasn't told me anything about sex yet. I guess it's because she thinks I am too young (I am twelve) or because she might feel embarrassed.

Ginny, age 12

Dear Judy,

I'm nine years old and in fourth grade. I think I might get my period soon. I have twenty-four-inch breasts and hair under my arms. Is that weird? To tell the truth I don't want it! I'm afraid to get my period very much. I don't want to be the first. My best friend says that I probably will be. She says that she has hair between her legs. Well, so do I. My mother got her period when she was ten.

Stephanie, age 9

Dear Judy,

Here is a problem. The boys in my class were making jokes about this girl because she had her period. And she got really upset. What I'm afraid of is that they might find out that I have my period too and if that happens then they won't stop making jokes about me and then the whole school will know about me. What should I do if that happens?

Also, when I need pads for my period I have trouble asking my mom to get the stuff and the first time I asked her she left the stuff lying on my bed. I was embarrassed that my dad might have seen the things. How can I ask my mom for the stuff so that I won't really be embarrassed?

Laurel, age 12

Dear Judy,

What would happen if I got my period in school? In the bathroom there is a machine that will give you a tampon or pad for ten cents, only I don't carry money around in my pocket. And I think that the machine is only for teachers.

Katie, age 10

Dear Judy,

Some people say they know *everything*. You're supposed to say that or the other kids think you're a child. I'm fourteen. I am ugly. I have pimples and no boyfriend. I am shy. I have never kissed a boy. I never talk about my period, not even to my mom or my best friend. Once, when I started at school I was really scared and I started to cry.

Jennifer, age 14

Parents and teachers should work together so that girls don't have to worry if they do get their periods at school. It always feels better to have a plan, to know what you are going to do in certain situations. At the beginning of each school year you could discuss this with your daughter so that she knows where pads or tampons are available, whether it's at the nurse's office, the machine on the wall in the girls' room, or even if a thoughtful teacher keeps a box in his or her classroom. That way she will feel reassured.

And don't forget to teach your sons about menstruation, too. If boys understood more about it, and about puberty in general, they wouldn't laugh. Boys who laugh do so out of their own embarrassment and lack of knowledge. We can help our kids—both boys and girls—feel more comfortable with each other by talking openly about the opposite sex.

Girls: If you get your period at school don't panic. When we were in seventh grade, my friend, Jane, got her first period at school. It happened during English class, while we were discussing *Ivanhoe*. Jane went to the girls' room and returned to class looking pale and worried.

"What's wrong?" I whispered.

"I think I got it," she said.

"You need help?" I asked.

"Yes," she said.

We asked the teacher if we could both be excused and explained that it was an emergency. She gave us permission and we went to the girls' room together. We bought a pad from the machine on the wall and I helped Jane pin it to her underpants. I thought she was very lucky to have started and I wondered if it would ever be my turn.

Dear Judy,

My name is Ruthann. I'm twelve and a half but I have a fourteen-year-old body. I have to ask you a very important question and I pray to God you answer my letter. You're my last hope. I have asked this to my school guidance counselor, along with the school nurse and they both told me I should be ashamed of myself.

You see, I told my mom I started my period a year ago and I really didn't. I really started just three months ago. Mom told me when I'm thirteen she would take me to a gynecologist. I've got two months to go before I turn thirteen. I'm afraid that the doctor will know I just started my period and he will tell my mom and I will get embarrassed so bad.

But I thought, if I tell her the truth now (knowing of course that doctors do have ways of finding out) I wouldn't be so embarrassed. But if they don't have ways of knowing I'm *not* going to tell her.

Do doctors have ways of finding out??? Please, please write to me and tell me.

Ruthann, age 12

Until I received Ruthann's letter I was sure I was the only one who had ever pretended to get her period. But I was so anxious to get mine that when I was in sixth grade and my friend, Rachel, began to menstruate I told her that I had started too. She didn't believe me. So the next day, in order to prove it to her, I wore the belt and one of the pads that I had asked my mother to buy for me (just in case) to school. Rachel still didn't believe me, so I took her hand, placed it on the bulky pad, and said, "Feel that!" She was surprised. I hoped she wouldn't ask to see further evidence.

During the morning Rachel complained about her menstrual cramps. I told her that I had them too. When our teacher asked us what we were talking about we went up to her desk and explained. She nodded and took us out into the hallway, where she taught us some exercises to relieve our cramps.

Lying about my period made me feel guilty and ashamed but I could see no way out without admitting what I had done. So I went on pretending to my friends that my periods had begun. I didn't tell my mother my secret. She hadn't started to menstruate until she was sixteen and I knew that I would probably be a late starter too.

Dear Judy,

I am a fourteen-year-old girl who hasn't gotten a period yet. My mother wants to take me to the doctor but I'm scared to go. I can't talk it over with my mother because we don't get along that well. I can't tell my dad anything because being an executive, he's never home and when I am with him I'm so glad to be with him that I forget there are things on my mind. I have two brothers and

three sisters, all older than me. Two of them
are married. So you see I'm rarely alone with
Dad.

I'm also worried because my mother is a nurse
and I think that she is keeping something from me
about it. I'm also scared because all of my friends,
when we do talk about it, say that a period is
really hectic, with putting in the tampons and
wearing the pads and all that. What should I
do?

Leigh, age 14

When I was fourteen and my periods still hadn't
started my mother took me to her gynecologist. We
didn't discuss the appointment in advance. My mother
picked me up at school one day and we drove to
Newark, to the doctor's office. It was raining. "What
will he do?" I asked my mother.

"Just talk to you and give you a checkup," she said.

"That's all?"

"Yes."

But the doctor didn't talk to me at all. He was very
stern. He told me to lie down on the table, he put my
feet in stirrups, and without warning, he examined me.
Now, a pelvic examination is nothing to be afraid of if
you're prepared and you understand what's going on.
And it doesn't hurt at all if you're relaxed. But no one
had told me anything about it and I was terrified. I felt
helpless and alone and the doctor did nothing to make
me feel more comfortable.

Afterward, even though the doctor said that nothing
was wrong, that I was normal, and that my periods
would begin soon, I was so angry and humiliated I cried

all the way home. I hated the doctor and I felt that my mother had betrayed me.

"Why didn't you tell me he would do that?" I finally asked her.

"I didn't want to frighten you," she said.

But there is nothing more frightening than not knowing.

Dear Judy,

My periods began just before my twelfth birthday, before any of my friends started, and for six months I suffered untold agonies that I was dying. I hid the evidence for fear it was something bad I had done. If your books had been around then I would have been spared all that. But then, my mother probably wouldn't have allowed me to read them.

Nadine, adult

I don't know any woman who doesn't remember her first period, and it is usually a much happier event than it was for Nadine. I finally got mine several months after my fourteenth birthday. I was spending the weekend with a friend from summer camp, at her family's home in Massachusetts. At first, I wasn't sure what the stain in my underpants was. When I realized it was my period I was elated! I asked my friend for a pad, but I didn't tell her or her mother that this was my first time. I wanted them to think I was experienced.

When Randy was thirteen, she and her friend, Allison, asked their Ouija boards when they would begin to menstruate. November 14 was the answer. They gathered the necessary equipment and waited for the big day. But November 14 came and went and nothing happened. A few months before Randy's fourteenth birthday she got her first period. I asked her about it recently.

Randy reminded me that she was at home when it happened. She says that I explained how to use a tampon because that's what she wanted to use. We also had pads in the house, just in case. But she was able to insert the tampon without difficulty. (I was not able to use a tampon until I was twenty-one.) She says she was happy to get her period but that it was no big deal. I remember crying. My daughter's first period made me feel very sentimental.

I think we should celebrate our first periods. That's why, when I was writing *Smart Women*, Michelle, seventeen, bakes a cake in honor of Sara, who is thirteen and has just had her first period. Even though these two girls have been thrown together by their parents' love affair, and there is a lot of tension and hostility between them, during that special moment of sisterhood, Michelle writes "Congratulations Sara!" on the icing on the cake.

A young friend of mine got her first period before her twelfth birthday, while she was traveling by herself, on a transcontinental flight. Her father met her in Africa and the first thing she said, after her long and arduous journey, was, "Dad . . . I got it!"

"Got what?" her father asked.

She couldn't believe that he didn't understand. "You know . . ." she told him.

"No, I don't," he said.

"Dad . . . I got my period!"

3

About Breast Development

Dear Judy,

Hi, my name is Emily. I am twelve years old and live in Kansas. In fifth grade I had a lot of boyfriends but now I am in seventh grade and I have none. It is because I am FLAT. All the boys tease me and call me "Board." Sometimes I feel like crying. All my friends talk about their periods and about shaving. I am afraid to ask my mother for a razor or a bra or a deodorant. One day I took my brother's deodorant so I would have some for gym.

What should I do about people teasing me and how should I ask my mother about a razor or bra? I can't even talk to my mother about getting my period. I learned about my period from my friends. My doctor said I am flat because I am very skinny. Please answer my questions fast.

Emily, age 12

Dear Judy,

I am flat and the boys make fun of me but I can't help it. They tease me so much I get stomachaches. They call me "Carpenter's Dream" (flat as a board) or "Pirate's Dream" (sunken treasure). One boy even calls me "Rolaids." They hurt my feelings so bad but I'm not going to cry in front of them. I don't want to tell my mom because I don't want her hurt because of this.

Meredith, age 12

When I was in the sixth grade I was flat-chested and had no bra. But on the morning of Field Day, a day of games and athletic events in our school yard, I stuffed two cotton balls into my T-shirt, just to find out what it would look like to have developed breasts, like many of my friends. My mother gave me an odd look that morning, but she didn't say anything.

In seventh grade I went shopping with my friend, Jane, and we each bought a bra, size 32 AA. I didn't need a bra but I wanted one. And then, at last, I had something to stuff. But I made the mistake of stuffing my bra with toilet paper and once, when I was dancing at the "Y" with a boy I really liked, he said, "What do you have in your bra . . . toilet paper?" And that was the end of that.

When I was in ninth grade I discovered padded bras and that summer, when I was fifteen, I went to a teen camp in Massachusetts, where, one sunny afternoon, the boys raided the girls' dorm and carried off our underwear. They took my padded bra, which had my name tape sewn inside, and they flew it, along with several other bras, also neatly name-taped, from the flagpole, for everyone to see.

A few of the girls went to their rooms and cried, but the rest of us laughed. Okay, our breasts were either too small or too large. And boys in groups could be stupid and insensitive. But there was nothing we could do about it.

Dear Judy,

I would like it if you could write about someone who is just the opposite of underdeveloped. *Overdeveloped*. Now, please don't think I'm trying to be pushy, I'm just suggesting . . .

Anyway, the reason I'm suggesting this is because I am a ten-year-old who looks more like a fourteen-year-old and I'm sure there are many others like me. And the underdeveloped would see, especially if you wrote it, how being overdeveloped isn't as easy as they think!

Betsy, age 10

I would gladly have traded places with the most developed girl in our sixth-grade class. Her name was Louise and we gave her a hard time because she developed earlier than the rest of us. I wrote the character of Laura Danker in *Are You There God? It's Me, Margaret* because for years I thought about how we had treated Louise. It pleased me, when in the book, Laura finally tells Margaret off, tells her how it feels to be the biggest in the class, the first to develop, and how it hurts when people make up stories about her just because she is an early bloomer. Now I know that we have no control over how early or late our bodies develop. But when I was young I hated being the smallest in the class and being teased about my flat chest was especially painful.

When Randy and Larry were in high school they gave me a T-shirt for my birthday. It said, *Flat is beautiful.* They weren't exactly sure how I would react, they told me later, and they hoped I wouldn't be insulted. I laughed over the T-shirt and wore it proudly.

Esther Hautzig, the author of *The Endless Steppe,* once told me that her friend had a well-developed daughter named Margaret. One day this woman saw her daughter standing in front of her mirror and she overheard her saying, "Are you there God? It's me, Margaret. Enough already!"

4

If Something Is Wrong

Dear Judy,

Hi! My name is Hayley. Even though my parents and I are very close I can't talk to them about sex and stuff like that. I think I can talk to you. Girls my age (nine) need someone to talk to. My big problem is my breasts. I noticed that for almost five months there are lumps in them. I can't tell Mom. I know you aren't a doctor but can you help? Also, I noticed that one breast is smaller than the other. It took guts to write this, so be a friend and help me, Judy!

Hayley, age 9

I have received other letters from girls who notice that one breast is developing faster than the other. Another girl wrote that she was worried about dark purple streak marks across her breasts. An eleven-year-old wrote about having a lot of hair under her lip. Her classmates were teasing her, saying, "You look like a hippie . . . you ought to shave." The girl said she felt like crying. She didn't know what to do.

For kids, suffering in silence and worrying about what *might* be wrong is worse than finding out the truth. Simple questions can be answered easily and reassuringly.

When I was a young teenager I caught impetigo, a skin disease that was going around in our school. In addition to having it on my face and on my scalp, I also had it *down there*.

On the night before my doctor's appointment I asked my father how I was going to tell the doctor that I had it in such a private place. My father told me the correct way to say it. The next day I went to the doctor and I told him that I also had it in my pubic hair. I felt myself turn purple as I said those words. But the doctor just nodded and said, "So you have it down there, too." He didn't make a big thing out of it. He helped me feel more comfortable.

A ten-year-old boy who had been in an accident and, as a result, had a scar on the side of his face, wrote to say that he was teased by his classmates at school. They called him "Scarface," "Pizza Face" and worse. But when his mother asked if the scar bothered him, he said no. He could not tell his mother the truth, he could not admit that the scar *did* bother him. It might have been better if his mother had said, "Would you like to find out if the doctor can do something about that scar?" That takes the burden off the child who might otherwise be embarrassed to discuss his or her problem.

Kids: If something is bothering you and your parents aren't aware of it, go to them. If you can't *ask* questions, you can't get answers.

5

About the Facts of Life

Dear Judy,
   Please send me the facts of life, in number
order.

Fern, age 9

As a child I knew that grown-ups kept secrets from me.
I hated those secrets. I had a million questions about
life but no one would tell me the answers. And most of
all, from the age of nine, I wanted information on
sexuality. I looked up *sex* in my *World Book Encyclopedia,* but all I found were pages and pages of overlays
about plants and how they reproduced. My frustration
at not being able to find the answers to my questions
was considerable.

   How sad that my parents never thought about buying
me a book about the facts of life. We were a book-
oriented family. We had a fine library where I would
browse for hours. No book was off limits to me. And

yet, the idea of buying me a book about human reproduction didn't occur to my parents. And it never occurred to me that I could ask for one.

Dear Judy,

I am eleven years old and my mom hasn't told me the facts of life yet. And I think I'm old enough to know them. Could you sort of be a second mother to me and tell me the facts of life?

Also, there is this boy in my class and his name is Eric and he is about the cutest boy in the whole school. Well, he asked me to go with him but I said no because when I would ask my mom she would probably laugh and say, "You don't even know the facts of life yet!" And then she would go and tell my dad and he would start teasing me. So what should I do?

Camille, age 11

Dear Judy,

My name is Bruce and I will be twelve soon. I would like to ask my parents a question but I don't know how. I would like to ask them about sex. How would I do it?

Bruce, age 11

Dear Judy,

Hi! My name is Beth. I'm twelve. I live in Longmeadow. I have a problem. You see, my mom hasn't told me one thing about sex, and we almost never talk. I really wish I had someone to talk to about things. Please don't write back and say I should ask my mom, because I really can't.

I have an older sister whom I love a lot. We are very close and I asked her to hint to my mom that I'm ready for her to give me the talk. But when I did my sister laughed. (She's nineteen.)

Please write back and help me!

Beth, age 12

Dear Judy,

Is it natural for a girl to be afraid to ask her mother about private subjects?

Suzy, age 11

Dear Judy,

I'm worried. I'm eleven and I've already learned that your period has something to do with feeding the baby when pregnant. I know I shouldn't worry but what would happen if I was pregnant and didn't have my period? Would the baby die? Could you send me a book to explain?

Erin, age 11

Dear Judy,

I know that there are a lot of mothers that are scared of talking to their children and the other way around. Do you have any special advice on how to talk to parents? If so could you drop me a line? When you were a child did you have trouble with talking to your mother?

Lydia, age 12

I'll say! My mother didn't talk to me about personal subjects at all. My father tried. Toward the end of the school year, when I was eleven, my father called me into his room. It was a balmy June night and I thought, from the serious tone of his voice, that I had done something wrong. But my father smiled as I approached him and said, "It's time we had a little talk."

"About what?" I asked.

"The birds and the bees," he said. "It's time for you to know how babies are made."

What followed was some sort of explanation about the seed and the egg and then something about intercourse. But by then I felt so embarrassed that I wasn't even listening.

"Oh, Daddy . . ." I said. "I already know about that."

"You do?" he said, surprised.

"Yes." I didn't really know that much about it. I had heard various stories at school. My friends and I talked about it a lot. My friend, Jane, got a lot of misinformation from her babysitter and she passed it on to us. But I didn't want to talk to my father about it. I just wanted to get out of that room.

I loved my father very much. I trusted him. I even appreciated the fact that he *tried* to tell me about sex. But I also knew, at eleven, that this was not going to work. I was going to have to get my information elsewhere. It was too difficult for him to tell me about sexuality or for me to ask him questions. It was too late. I had already learned that my earliest questions made my parents so uncomfortable that I had stopped asking them.

I'm not blaming my parents for not talking with me about sex. They came from a generation that didn't know how to discuss personal subjects with kids.

Dear Judy,

I am thirty-one years old and have two children —a girl, six, and a boy, two. I hope to have an open, trusting relationship with my children, no matter what their ages. During my last pregnancy I feel I was quite honest and open with my daughter concerning our bodies and the birth process, but when she asked, "How did the baby get into your uterus?" all I could say was, "Mommy and Daddy love each other very much and wanted the baby there."

One day she and her brother will ask again and this won't be an appropriate answer. What do I say? You see, my problem is, I can't imagine myself speaking of intercourse with my kids, although I feel I should and deep down I really want to. I can't imagine myself being comfortable with direct methods.

I'm also afraid my kids will sense my nervousness and not come to me with their questions.

Please arm me with something to say!

Thanks.

Vera, adult

When I had children I vowed that they would never have to go elsewhere for information about sexuality. I vowed that I would answer every question my children asked, honestly and to the point. And so, I could not believe how my heart pounded on the morning that my five-year-old daughter took an egg from the refrigerator, carried it to the corner of the kitchen, squatted over it, and announced that she was going to make a baby. I remember the scene clearly. I was preparing breakfast and Larry, who was two and a half, was dancing all around the kitchen, singing, "Randy's going to make a baby . . . Randy's going to make a baby . . ."

This is it, I thought. And so, with sweaty palms and a dryness in my mouth, I told them that humans don't make babies that way. I explained briefly how humans do make babies. And as I did I felt an enormous sense of relief. It was so easy. It was just as easy as talking about the pancakes I was making.

That afternoon I stopped at the bookstore and bought a copy of *How Babies Are Made*. My children and I shared that book many times in the next few years. Like any shared experience, books can bring people closer together.

When Larry was in fourth grade he had a friend who believed that God sprinkled dust on his mother's belly button and that was how he was conceived. When he found out the truth he was angry. And who can blame him? I've often wondered if he will grow up to tell his children the same ridiculous story.

Years ago I was working on a booklet about menstruation and I asked a group of young, married professional men with children—"What is a uterus?" Not one of them could actually define a uterus. Not one of them could say, that's the place inside a woman's body, also known as the womb, where the baby grows. They didn't know because no one had told them. And they had not taken the time to find out on their own. What are these men going to tell their children?

I hope they're going to make an effort to break the cycle. I hope they're going to say, "I want to be able to talk to my kids about sex. I want them to come to me with their questions. So I'm going to get ready."

But, even if you're determined, you still might feel uncomfortable, or even inadequate, at first. That's okay. Once you have your information and feel comfortable with the presentation in the books or other materials you've selected to share with your kids, you'll learn to relax. If your kids are very young, hold them close while you're reading to them, so they can see that it's not a frightening idea, but a loving one. If your kids are older you might hand them a book and tell them if they have any questions to come to you. It's never too late to begin. It's better to give your kid a book at fourteen than never to have given one at all.

Sex education isn't a one-shot deal. It's not one session with the school nurse, one film shown in sixth grade, or one conversation about the birds and the bees. Like growing up, it is an ongoing process.

Kids: If you need information, ask your parents to help you find a book that will explain puberty and human reproduction. Sometimes it will be up to you. You can't wait around, like I did, hoping that your parents will bring home that book. You have to tell them that you need it. You may have to help your parents feel comfortable. But if everybody is too embarrassed, both parents and kids, we're going to raise another generation of frightened, uncomfortable, sexually ignorant people.

6

About Masturbation

Dear Judy,

   I have read all of your books. They help me not to be afraid and they answer my questions. I thought I was different but I'm not. In your books are things I would never bring out in the open with my mother. Like in your book *Deenie*—she touches her special place. Well, I do that too, but I always thought I was the only one.

Jolene, age 13

Dear Judy,

   My mom and I have a very open relationship. But the one thing I cannot bring myself to mention to anyone is masturbation. I know (and your books helped me to understand) that it's not bad. Just something about it is really embarrassing.

Barbara, age 14

Dear Judy,

I want to ask you a very important question. Okay, I'll start from the beginning. When I was little, about four or five, I started touching my special place. And I got a nice feeling. I had a baby-sitter during this time. Her name was Donna. And she knew that I touched my special place. She said that if I kept touching it, it would get big, then it would bleed, then it would fill with pus and pop! Then I would have to have an operation. So I stopped touching it.

When I was going into sixth grade I started again. And one day this stuff came out of me. My mom said it was discharge and that it's normal. But I'm scared to even touch my special place now. I think it *will* pop. This is serious. I told my mom and she told me that Donna was just lying but I'm still scared. Can you explain what happened? Please answer this letter as I am very scared.

Heather, age 12

Yes, there are still myths about masturbation! The stories that Donna told Heather were frightening and destructive. A grown man wrote that his adolescent years were "a quiet hell of silent suffering." He said that he thought it was the fact that nobody ever talked about masturbation that led him to believe that he was the only disgusting, degenerate pervert in the world.

I never heard the word masturbation when I was growing up. Yet at twelve I knew I had a special place and that I could get that good feeling by touching it. I talked about it with some of my friends, who had also discovered that they had special places. I never found anything relating to my early sexuality in books, so there was some comfort in finding out from my friends that I was not alone.

Dear Judy,

I read your book *Deenie.* You wouldn't believe how happy I was to know that I'm not the only person to do what Deenie does. You are the only person who has ever mentioned anything about this. So could you please answer my questions.

1. How did you find out about this?
2. Is it a kind of disease?
3. How did *I* know to start doing this?
4. Am I weird?
5. How many other letters have you received saying that other people do this (if any)?
6. Approximately how many people do this?
7. Is what I do going to harm my insides (like by not letting me have children)?
8. Am I a fag?

I hope to hear from you very soon. Please!

Nikki, age 13

When you are choosing books about sexuality for your kids make sure that there is an honest discussion of masturbation included. Chances are, they're not going to want to talk about it with you, but just finding out that it's okay will be a relief to them.

A young man wrote that he didn't get a good night's sleep during his adolescent years. He tried to train his mind before he went to sleep to think about mathematical problems. He tried to concentrate on them so he wouldn't have erections, or worse, wet dreams.

When *Then Again, Maybe I Won't* was published I met a woman who told me that her son had been given a copy for his twelfth birthday. She read the book first but before giving it back to him she cut out two pages. "How did you do that?" I asked. "With a scissors," she said. When I asked why she had cut out those two pages she told me that she didn't think her son was old enough to read about wet dreams or masturbation.

Last year I met her son. He is twenty-four now. I asked him if he remembered the book. "Sure," he said. "And I always knew that my mother had cut out those pages even though she told me it was a printing error. So I went down to the public library and I read the rest of the book there."

7

About Same-Sex Crushes and Homosexuality

Dear Judy,

I am close to my mother but not my father. However, sex is not an open subject with us. Would you do me a favor and consider writing a book about how homosexuality becomes involved in good friends at grades four through eight. It isn't something that will stick but it does happen. Thanks.

Ned, age 14

Dear Judy,

I like boys but I think I am gay! Please don't think I am just thinking that. I do believe I am gay.

Polly, age 11

Dear Judy,

I am a girl in seventh grade and I have a funny feeling about one of my teachers. I am afraid I might be in love with her or something. My friend says she feels that way about her cousin. I'll bet a lot of girls—and boys—feel this way. Could you please write a book about it?

Thank you.

P.S. You don't have to. Maybe it is only me who feels this way.

Margo, age 13

Dear Judy,

When I was about twelve I noticed that I was feeling toward girls the way most girls begin feeling about boys. I had no label to put on it and *certainly* no one to talk to about it. It was tormenting, horrible, and I kept trying to cover it up and hoping one day I would miraculously find a boy I could feel the same way about. I was desperate to find The Boy who would change me and save me from this awful thing. Of course, I never did.

Anyway, for the sake of a lot of young kids out there who think they're the only ones in the whole world, would you consider writing a book about this.

Joanne, adult

Like Joanne, other adults have written sharing their experiences and urging me to write a book about a young person who is gay. A man in his thirties wrote that when he was young, he felt "despairingly lonely."

190

There was no one he could talk to about his feelings. He searched bookstores, hoping to find a book that would let him know he was all right. Another man wrote poignantly about having denied himself the joy of young romance. He still does not know how to tell his family he is gay. He is afraid they will reject him.

Because I tend to write out of my own experiences and feelings I don't know if I will ever write that book. But others have written about being gay and will again. I hope parents will remember that early same-sex crushes, sexual play and experimentation do not necessarily mean that a person is homosexual. What is most important is to prevent young people from feeling judged or condemned for their feelings and to encourage them to feel good about themselves, no matter what their sexual preference.

Chapter VIII
BOYS AND GIRLS TOGETHER

1

Who Doesn't Want to Be Popular?

Dear Judy,

I am a thirteen-year-old girl. I'm in eighth grade. Do you think thirteen is too young to date? My parents think it is. All my friends have been going out since seventh grade at least. I haven't even been asked to go out once. I'm very studious. I read nine or ten books a week. I get the best grades in school. People really don't associate with me much. Kids seem to think I'm a snob. I'm really not. I'd do anything to be popular. What do you suggest?

Shona, age 13

Who doesn't want to be popular? Being popular means being accepted by the "Right People," the "In Group," the ones who have all the fun. It means never being left out or lonely, never having to worry about being invited to parties, and success with the opposite sex. At least that's what I thought when I was growing up.

My mother wanted me to be popular, maybe because she had been too shy as a girl to be a part of the popular crowd at her school. Some parents hope their children will live out their dreams and they lead their kids to believe they will be disappointed if they don't come through. I felt a lot of pressure to be popular so I kept the *real* me hidden, deep inside. I never confided my worries, my fears, my insecurities or disappointments, to my family or my friends. Instead, I clowned around and flirted with the boys. I knew exactly how to get attention.

But the summer I was fifteen (the same summer that my grandmother died) I went to a teen camp with my friend, Rachel. Neither one of us knew anyone else at the camp. Within a week Rachel had been accepted by the popular crowd and I had not. For the first time I knew what it was like to be an outsider. I felt isolated and alone. Rachel and I went our own ways that summer and our friendship was never the same after that. I never did admit to my parents that I was unhappy that summer, that I was counting the days until I could go home. If they knew it was a difficult time for me, they didn't say.

My father used to warn my mother that if my brother and I didn't experience pain and disappointment we would never develop strong characters. We wouldn't grow up feeling sympathetic to others. My mother wanted us to be happy all the time. I am still trying to convince her that it isn't possible to be happy all the time.

Dear Judy,

Your books have helped me through my almost twelve years of life. There is one problem, however, that they have not quite solved. I am not very popular and this one girl, whom I find very hard to stand, is, though I don't know why. She's already had her period (I haven't) and is always brushing her hair. How can I become more popular? I think if I was better at sports and P.E. I might have friends who would like me better. I don't know.

Melissa, age 12

Dear Judy,

I am in eighth grade. What I wanted to ask you about is popularity. I am reasonably pretty and a nice person, I think, but no guy calls me or talks to me a whole lot. I've never been on a date or held hands or anything!

Nancy, age 14

Dear Judy,

I have some problems. They are that my friend, Yvonne, is ugly and looks like a boy. But she has gone with seven guys in one year. I'm not ugly and I don't look like a boy. So I'm wondering, why is she so popular? And how come she gets all the boys and I don't?

Arianna, age 12

Dear Judy,

Whenever my mom asks if I had a good time at a party I always say yes, even if it was rotten. I feel I can't confide in her. I am going to raise my children openly so they feel they have a friend in me. I will always raise them truthfully!

Kathy, age 13

That letter brings back so many memories. When I was young and came home from parties or dances I always answered my mother's questions with the words I thought she wanted to hear rather than the truth.

"Were you the most popular girl at the dance?" she would ask. Often I wanted to shout, No . . . no . . . I had a terrible time. But I felt I couldn't be honest with her about my feelings. I felt that she would be disappointed in me.

As a parent I struggled with these issues again as I watched my shy daughter, who also longed for popularity, grow up. But we don't have the power to make our kids popular. We have nothing to say about how other kids feel about them. All we can do is try to help them feel good about themselves. So praise them often, and with honesty. Help them learn to value the positive side of others and of themselves. As I experienced my children's pain and disappointments secondhand, I tried to remember what my father said—that if everything goes right all of the time as you're growing up, you're not very well prepared for life.

Kids: There is no magic formula for popularity. Even the most popular kids can be insecure. Some of them work so hard at being popular that they lose sight of everything else. It took me years to learn that I didn't have to apologize for having nothing to do over the weekend and that I wasn't a failure if my social calendar wasn't booked weeks in advance. The only advice I can offer is that natural, friendly behavior goes a long way. It's a lot easier to accept other people if you also accept yourself. In the long run self-esteem is more important than popularity.

2

Crushes

Dear Judy,

I wish someone would write a book about what I'm going through. My name is Courtney. I'm eleven years old and in sixth grade. I knew that I would hate school this year and I'm right. The guy that I had a crush on since third grade is in a different school now because he's a year older than me. So I never get to see him. One of my best friends hates me now. She thinks I'm trying to steal her boyfriend just because I'm always talking to him. Another problem that I have is that I cry easily. I get so angry! I don't know what it is that makes me that angry. I don't know what it is that makes me cry either.

Courtney, age 11

During my first few years of elementary school my best friend was a boy, Harvey. I ate freshly picked carrots from his garden, played in his basement on rainy days, learned to ride a two-wheeler bicycle beside him and walked to and from school with him every day.

In fifth grade our friendship changed. We were still friendly, but we weren't close anymore. He went around with the boys and I went around with the girls. It was boys against girls that year, but in a new and exciting way. In sixth grade it was no longer boys *against* the girls. Now we were curious about each other in a different way. The girls talked romantically about the boys. We kept "lists" under our desk blotters, "lists" of which boys we liked and in what order. By junior high I was in love (or thought I was) with a different boy every other week. But I was really in love with the idea of love.

My parents treated my crushes with respect. They made my friends of both sexes welcome at our house. As I grew up my friends envied me because my parents encouraged me to bring my boyfriends home. I never had to park on a dark road to be alone with a boy. I was assured privacy at home. When I had kids I also wanted them to feel that our house was open to their friends.

I remembered my own early crushes as I watched Randy and Larry experience the joy of returned affection and the pain of rejection. Larry usually wanted to talk about it. Randy kept most of her thoughts and feelings on the subject to herself. I tried to respect her privacy because I had hated it when my mother questioned me endlessly after every date. Still, I wanted to let her know I was there for her. But there are times when the last thing kids want is to talk to their parents about their private lives.

Dear Judy,
    I really like a boy named Ellis as a boyfriend. He likes me, at least a little, but as a "friend." I sit

in front of him in homeroom. We're getting a new seating chart though and we are going to be separated because we talk too much. Many other girls like him too, including a skinny 34C (I'm a fat 34B). I don't see him out for recess and now I won't even see him in class. How can I make him like me?

Pat, age 13

Dear Judy,

I am sick and tired of my mother. She never lets me do anything. I've tried ignoring her but she just yells at me more. Then sometimes I cry and she gets mad.

I have this friend, Matthew. At the beginning of the year I thought Matthew was a real jerk. Now I love him. My mom, dad and sisters *think* I love him but I don't want them to know I really do.

When Matthew is around other people he treats me like dirt. It makes me feel bad. I really want to tell him I love him but I don't know how to tell him. How should I? I mean, he's not the kind you can hold hands with when you walk down the street. I really want him to love me, too.

Allison, age 12

Dear Judy,

I've liked this guy, Jeff, since the beginning of the year. He used to like me but he's not allowed to like girls anymore. Now, even though I still like him, I am going with Bill. But I kind of like this other Bill, too, and also Kevin. The Bill I'm going with is thirteen, the other Bill is fourteen and Kevin is sixteen. Still, I like Jeff the best, even though he can't like me. I feel that I'll always like him a lot. I think about him all the time. I'm all confused. I don't know what to do anymore. Do you have any advice for me?

Morgan, age 13

Dear Judy,
   I am thirteen-and-a-half years old and my problem is, I can't seem to find the right boy for me. There is a boy named Martin that wants me to be his girlfriend but I just want to be his "friend." The right boy for me would be at least fifteen, sixteen, or seventeen. He would have pretty eyes, dark hair, a nice build and soft skin. He would show me love and he would respect me, himself and others. He would have his license, maybe. But boys like this don't come around here. I really need help. I want someone to love besides family.

Sasha, age 13

We all have our romantic fantasies but Sasha's sounds good to me. At least she cares about respect. When I was young my romantic fantasies came from the movies. I saw *Ruby Gentry* seven times when I was in eighth grade. That year I invited a ninth-grade boy, Dick, to go to a party with me. He accepted my invitation and for weeks all I could think about was how it would be between us. I would dress in blue jeans and a black sweater like Jennifer Jones and Dick would sweep me off my feet like Charlton Heston. Even though there was no swamp in suburban New Jersey, I pictured us walking through the woods, hand in hand, stopping to kiss at every tree.

On the night of the party it rained and my father had to drive us. When we got there Dick didn't even dance with me. He just hung out with the other guys. And later, when we said goodnight, he didn't try to kiss me. In fact, he acted as if he couldn't wait to be rid of me. I cried myself to sleep for nights.

A few years ago I met Dick again and as we were reminiscing I asked him if he remembered that party. He didn't. I told him how disappointed I had been that he wasn't romantically interested in me. He was surprised. "I was only interested in basketball then," he told me. "I didn't care anything about girls until I was sixteen."

So much for romantic fantasies!

3

Kisses

Dear Judy,

How does a girl kiss a boy—arms around the neck or waist? Also, do you squeeze the lips real hard and are the girl's lips placed exactly on the boy's or is the girl's upper lip above the boy's upper lip or what?

Melanie, age 11

Dear Judy,

I do feel kind of ridiculous writing this letter but really I am drastic for help. I am fourteen and I have a problem! I know it's crazy but it's really got me worried. My mother and I are close. She told me everything she believes I should know! And plus, if I do have any questions I could ask my older sisters. So I consider myself lucky.

They tell me everything but leave out one thing, which I consider very important. The simple, beautiful kiss. Consider as you like, but I am fourteen and have never had a real down-to-earth kiss! It's not that I'm ugly or have "cooties" or anything but I want my first kiss to be perfect. Sure, I've had your little lip touches, but nothing real. I've asked my sisters how a kiss is done but they just say, "Oh, it will come natural when the time comes." I'm sick of everyone telling me this.

Could you tell me how to kiss? I really need someone I could ask this to without giving me the same old answer. Please help me out and try to reply as soon as possible and I will be deeply in your debt.

Maggie, age 14

Dear Judy,

I first started a kind of relationship with a girl in a movie. We just saw each other there by coincidence so we sat together. The next thing you know we were holding hands. Before we left the theater she stood on her tiptoes and kissed me. I'd never been so red at the face in my life. But if that's what falling in love feels like I hope it happens to everybody!

Greg, age 12

Dear Judy,

I am a boy, twelve, almost thirteen. I know you're no "Dear Abby" but still maybe you can help me. I met a girl from New Jersey. My mom let me take her out to lunch. The next day we had her over to our house for dinner. The day after that I went to the house where she was staying. We knew each other one week then and before she went back to New Jersey we both wanted to kiss. We kept saying we were going to do it but then we never did. I guess we both weren't sure about it. So we agreed on the next time. But what if the same thing happens then?

Brad, age 12

Dear Judy,

I need some advice. I'm a big romantic but so far I'm convinced that there is no such thing as "true love." I've gone with a lot of boys over the last two years and I'm really confused. For one thing, in movies they make kissing look so perfect, but it's not for me. In fact, we slobber all over each other and we always end up getting the flu. Not that I don't like kissing but like I said, I'm a romantic and I want it to be special.

Only once did a boy tell me that he loved me, and I loved him, or at least I thought I did. Will I ever feel something special when I kiss boys? I want to but I'd rather just hug them or sit close to them, nestled in their arms. Is there something wrong with me? I wish I could have true love. I'm so confused. I am fourteen years old. I want you to help me.

Krista, age 14

Kids: No one can teach you to kiss. It's something you learn on your own. But you don't have to worry about making mistakes because there are no rules when it comes to kissing. Whatever feels good is okay. Try not to worry about it, try not to get so anxious and tense that you don't give yourself a chance to enjoy it.

We played kissing games at parties in sixth grade but the kisses were just pecks on the cheek. In seventh grade I used to practice kissing my pillow. My first kiss finally came toward the end of seventh grade. It happened at a party where we were playing "Post Office." I was so nervous and so unsure of what to do that I couldn't stop laughing.

By eighth grade we were going to kissing parties regularly. And that was *all* we did. *Kiss, kiss, kiss.* We played a game called "Rotation," where the girls moved from boy to boy as the music changed—our new version of musical chairs. I got a lot of kissing practice that year, but after a while the game became boring. Also, I discovered that *just* kissing isn't nearly as nice as kissing someone you really like.

4

How Far to Go

Dear Judy,

I am twelve years old and loaded with problems. A boy asked me to neck. If I say no, he'll get mad at me. So I got scared and went to my sister and asked her what to do. She said, "Well, if you want to, go ahead." I wanted to but didn't know how so I practiced on my Shaun Cassidy posters but that didn't help because the boy wanted to "French." So we broke up.

Now there's another boy and I necked with him once and he got mad because that wasn't enough for him so I had to drop him. Now when I try to talk to my sister she has a fit. And I can't talk to my mom because I have tried many times and she just says to call those boys *pigs!*

Denise, age 12

Dear Judy,

I've never had the courage to write you before but I'm doing it now. It seems like I have something in common in every book of yours I've read. I'm now fourteen and haven't started my period. It worries and scares me but I haven't got anyone to talk to. My little brother and I are now the only children at home. My sister is in college and my older brother lives in New Mexico. My parents separated when I was in fifth grade. I've lived with Mom and her live-in, then Dad. That was okay. But after Daddy got married it was Daddy and my brother and me *plus* my stepmom and my stepsisters. Things just didn't work out when Daddy wasn't home so my brother and I moved back in with Mom after she married her live-in.

Boys are a problem and so is virginity. I like boys but will not go far. Most people at school think you are weird if you are in the eighth grade and a virgin. I think it is something I want to save for marriage. A boy likes me and wants me to go to the movies with him but Mom won't let me go. What shall I do? She's the kind of person you can't sit down and talk to. I've tried.

All my feelings build up inside of me because I can't talk about it with my mom and I'm too shy to do so with my friends. I think I am overweight but do not know. Judy, give me some advice or just write to me. I'm very lonely and haven't got anyone to talk to. Sometimes I just go to my room and cry.

Stacey, age 14

When I was growing up we had very firm rules about how far to go. Nice girls didn't go all the way. We were supposed to be virgins until we were safely married. I guess not all of us were though, because in my senior class two girls, both of them honor students, both of them on their way to college, had to drop out of school and get married because they were pregnant. In the fifties abortion was illegal. I've often wondered what happened to those girls. Surely their lives were changed forever because they became pregnant while they were in high school.

Times have changed. Kids today have to make many more decisions on their own. As parents we can help them learn to make those decision wisely. We can acknowledge today's realities without giving up our own values, not by hiding from the issues, but by facing them and talking about them with our kids. Find out what your kids think by talking with them about characters in books and movies. That's an easier way for both of you to say what's on your minds. It's also easier if you remember that times have changed, but feelings haven't. We can't control our kids' behavior but we can share our views on what's right for our family, and why.

Dear Judy,

I had a boyfriend. Even though we only made out a little it meant a lot to me. It broke my heart when I found out that he was just using me. I loved him very much. I don't mean this to sound like the *Late Show* but that's how it was. I've never told anybody this before. I hope I haven't bored you with my letter but I just had to tell somebody.

Rachel, age 11

Dear Judy,

I just broke up with my boyfriend. I still lose sleep over him. But my family doesn't understand. They say, "Caroline . . . why do you lose sleep over him? He's not worth it." How can I tell them that we made love off and on? And that when I was with him I felt so warm and safe. Maybe this sounds dumb, writing my love life to you, but I thought maybe you could write a book about us.

Caroline, age 13

Sometimes parents send their kids mixed messages. We tell them to do one thing but act as if we want them to do another. We confuse them. Some kids wish their parents would set sexual limits. "Intercourse is a lot to handle at an early age. Wait until you're out of high school." Randy might have appreciated that.

Larry says he would have found such advice condescending. He preferred discussions focusing on sexual facts and responsibility. Had I set up any hard and fast rules regarding his sexual behavior he might not have come to me with his questions. There are no easy answers. So much depends on family values, emotional maturity and life experiences.

Many girls tell me that they rarely enjoy early intercourse. They do it to please their boyfriends. Well, it's nice to do things for someone you care about, but intercourse shouldn't be one of them. I don't believe in a double standard—but I do think we can encourage kids to enjoy their sexuality without early intercourse.

I know kids of both sexes who go off to college

feeling like failures because they are still virgins. They get there and are so anxious to get it out of the way that they have intercourse with the first person who comes along and it is usually a disappointing experience.

A high school girl I know, Shelley, sleeps with everyone. She uses sex to prove that she is lovable and worthy. A young woman, Pat, wrote that she had been taught it was wrong to respond sexually. She held back for so long that it is now difficult for her to relax and enjoy making love with her husband. She says, "I hope I will be lucky enough to unlearn those automatic stop signs that were unnaturally placed in my mind, but many my age have already passed that moldable stage." She is twenty-one and has been married for two years.

We all want our kids to grow up with healthy attitudes toward making love. We don't want them to use sex to prove they are worthy, like Shelley. We want them to be able to learn to say no as easily as okay and to feel good about their decision, without becoming so anxious that they can't respond sexually at all, like Pat. We also have to make them aware of sexually transmitted diseases. Most of all we want them to learn to be responsible about sex.

Kids: Never do anything you don't want to do. Never let anyone pressure you into behavior or actions you're not ready for, anything that doesn't feel right for you, whether it's sexual or not.

Dear Judy,
  I am a fourteen-year-old girl who likes to be in style and if a special style comes out I have to be

in it. In my area there are a lot of fine guys and I know almost all of them. A lot of the guys like me 'cause of my body but most like me for my personality.

I like to go to jams and parties and get high with them. I hang out a lot. My mom doesn't let me hang out late so in order to be with a guy around here it has to be on a weekend. Sometimes I cut out of school. I know it's not right but I like to feel loved by a guy. I like to be squeezed, hugged and kissed by a guy and the only way to be with a guy like that is to cut out of school.

In the summer I used to leave my job at lunchtime to be with this guy named Sean. He is so fine! All the girls are after him. Half of the girls in this area have made it with him. The guys around here always have more than one girl. I'm still a virgin. Most of my friends aren't. I do often think of having sex but I really don't want to have it 'cause I don't want to wind up with a bad reputation like some of my friends. A lot of guys tried to get me to have sex with them but I stop them.

Tiffany, age 14

I wrote the book *Forever* . . . , the story of Katherine and Michael, seniors in high school, when Randy was fourteen. She asked if I could write about two nice kids who fall in love, do it, and nothing terrible happens to them. Randy had read a number of books that year that linked sex with punishment. If a girl succumbed she would wind up with a grisly abortion, abandonment and a life ruined. I think Randy was bothered by the message of those books in which boys never had any feelings and were only interested in using girls. And neither boys nor girls ever felt responsible for their actions.

In *Forever . . .* , Katherine's mother says, "Sex is a commitment . . . once you're there you can't go back to holding hands." I can remember my father saying to me, "I hope you'll wait until you're twenty-five or married . . . whichever comes first." Today I don't know anyone of twenty-five who would admit to being a virgin. Since I was married at twenty-one I never had to make that decision.

But kids today do have to make decisions about their sexuality and too many of them still lack the information they need to decide intelligently. The highest incidence of unwanted pregnancy in this country occurs from the ages of fourteen to seventeen. Kids don't have a clear understanding of what teenage pregnancy and parenthood really means, economically or emotionally. Some girls say they did not even know they could become pregnant the first time they had intercourse.

A sixteen-year-old, Robin, told me she would not think of being the one to get or to use birth control devices or products because then it would look as if she'd planned to have intercourse. She had to believe that she gave in only because her boyfriend insisted. Another girl, Lisa, uses abortion as her method of birth control. She has already had two abortions and she is just eighteen. These kids are not thinking responsibly about sex and adults are not talking with them about the issues early enough.

Dear Judy,
    After reading *Forever . . .* I can really see that my relationship with Adam may not be like it is

now, forever. That book can really make you think. I only wish I had read it sooner. Maybe I would have held off when it came to sex with Adam.

Kim, age 17

Dear Judy,
  It was the same way for my boyfriend, Don, and me as it was in your book *Forever* . . . As it is, we will be getting married next month. I read parts of your book to Don, the parts I didn't quite understand. It made it easier for us to talk about sex.

Tanya, age 19

Dear Judy,
  It's about midnight here and I just finished reading your book *Forever* . . . I was involved like Michael, in the book. She and I were together for six months and we were engaged and then something happened and she fell out of love with me. I tried to kill myself but at the last minute I made myself throw up the pills I had taken.
  Then I heard about your book. It really helped me see that the six months with her were the best six months of my life. I no longer feel like killing myself because I realize that no one can take my memories away from me. You made me see how much there is to live for.

Daniel, age 19

Dear Judy,

I have a friend, Andrea. When she was fourteen she got pregnant. Her parents kicked her out. She got an apartment with her boyfriend. When he found out she was pregnant he left her. Now she's fifteen, due any day and living by herself. Do you have any ideas on how I could help her? And please, would you hurry? Thank you.

Jessica, age 15

A sixteen-year-old girl, Melissa, wrote to say that her friend was pregnant and had decided to have the baby. Melissa, who is unhappy at home, thought her friend, Jill, was really lucky to be marrying her boyfriend, who has a job, a truck, an apartment and dental insurance. Melissa wished that it would happen to her, too.

In her next letter, Melissa wrote to say that Jill had married her boyfriend and now she and Jill weren't as close as they used to be. "We can't be. Her hubby won't let her do anything. She can't go to the mall with me unless he comes too. She can't come over to my house. I already see her messing up just by putting up with that. She can't *breathe* without him. Even when he's working he won't let her spend any time with me."

Jill's baby isn't due for several months, but Melissa already sees that the romantic married life she imagined is far from realistic.

Kids: Both boys and girls should be responsible for preventing unwanted pregnancies. If you're worried about spontaneity, about romance, about just letting whatever happens, happen—then you're not mature enough to handle intercourse. It's up to you to take control. It's your body. It's your life.

In *Forever* . . . Katherine's mother gives her an article from *The New York Times* that asks the following questions:

1. Is sexual intercourse necessary for the relationship?
2. What should you expect from sexual intercourse?
3. If you should need help, where will you seek it?
4. Have you thought about how this relationship will end?

If you do decide to have intercourse use birth control. Go to a doctor or a family-planning clinic before you do it. It only takes one time to get pregnant or to make someone pregnant. And ask yourself if you're ready emotionally too. How will you feel if it doesn't last? How will you feel if the next day you see him or her with someone else? Will it still have been worth it? Will you have regrets?

It's wonderful to be in love, to discover sexual attraction, but that doesn't mean you can't *think* anymore. There is no one right answer for everyone, but feeling pressured, feeling that you have to do it because everyone else does, or that you will lose him or her if you don't—that's not the way to start out your life of sexual responsibility.

Chapter IX
TROUBLE IN THE FAMILY

1

Foster Care

Dear Judy,
 I like to roller-skate, do gymnastics and read. I live in a group home with thirteen other kids. It is called the Haven. We have school every day from nine to three. In the summertime we go swimming and have summer school and go on field trips to different places. We have counselors in this place. I have problems that I have to work on here. After I get done working on my problems I will go to a family.

Carla, age 12

In 1977 I gave a talk at a convention of reading teachers and after, when I asked for questions, a woman stood and chided me for never having written about kids in detention centers, group homes or foster care. With emotion she talked about working with kids who, for one reason or another, cannot live with their families. I tried to explain that no one author can write about every situation and that most of us write out of our own experiences. I told her that maybe one of the kids she works with will grow up to write that book.

Dear Judy,

I am from a broken home and in foster care. I have not seen or heard from my dad since I was two. I'm seventeen now. There have been times in the last few years that the only way I knew I wasn't strange was because you told me in your books that feeling lonely, rejected and scared were okay feelings. To release my feelings I write, mainly poetry.

Like you, I want to write what I wish someone had written for me to read. For instance, I have only read two books about kids in foster homes and those books only told about small kids. Teenagers who are in foster care and have been moved around feel totally different but no one will discuss it or get near the subject. Why? I want so much to let other kids know they are not the only people with various feelings, like you let us know.

Here is one of my poems:

THE MAN WHO ISN'T THERE

My father is a man that I do not know
Except for the things I have heard.
I dream of him but I cannot see his face.
I know he talks but I cannot hear his words.
I see his presence but cannot feel his warmth.
I dream of him but I cannot share his feelings.

I see him reach out but I cannot feel his touch.
I reach into my dream but he is no longer there.

Meg, age 17

Dear Judy,
Well, hi! I'm an eighth-grade student living in a 'boys' home," away from my real home and not knowing what is going on there and worrying if it is safe to call home and find out.

So what I wrote to ask is if you could write a book about the same situation. The mother is working two part-time jobs, trying to make ends meet for all. There is a fifteen-year-old boy and a fourteen-year-old boy. The fourteen-year-old is living in this "boys' home" away from the fifteen-year-old who is living at the real home, trying to fill in for the father's position.

The father is living in the same town, also working two jobs and wanting, after sixteen years of marriage, to finally love and take part in the family. The fourteen-year-old is in the middle and the only person *he* can talk to is his uncle.

If you can't write a book about this could you give me some advice?

Ben, age 14

I am always amazed at the ability children have to cope and survive. Like everyone else, these troubled kids wish they had someone to talk to, someone to tell them the facts. It is *not* knowing what is going to happen to them that is the hardest.

2

Runaways

Dear Judy,

I am ten and in fifth grade. I am very sad because my sister ran away from home. Her name is Naomi and she is sixteen. All we know is that she met this boy and she fell in love with him. We think this boy put her up to running away. She has been gone almost nine weeks.

I know you can write a very good story about me and my sister and how much I wish she would come home.

Barry, age 10

My stepdaughter has friends who have run away. But running away doesn't solve anything. Running away is a symptom, not a solution. Instead, families have to sit down together and face the facts. They have to deal with reality. Only then can they make the changes that will help them live together in peace. And often they need help in doing that.

My brother ran away once. He was about eighteen and had failed a couple of college courses. When his grades came he and my father had a long late-night talk. The next morning my brother was gone. He had taken the family car.

What followed was one of the longest days of my life, and I'm sure it was for my parents, and my brother, too. I hated my brother that day. I hated him for the pain he was causing our family. I hated him because I saw my father break down and sob, blaming himself. I hated him because I felt that I would somehow have to explain his behavior to friends, who would ask about him. Why couldn't he just be like everyone else? I wondered. Why did he have to have so many problems?

Late that afternoon a telegram arrived from David. "I'm thinking hard," it said. That evening he phoned to say he was coming home. My parents rejoiced. It was very late when he finally did get home. I had fallen asleep on the sofa in the living room, waiting for him. I was glad to see him, but I thought the hero's welcome was out of place. Was I jealous? Did I resent the attention focused on him? Maybe.

I don't know if my parents ever talked to David about that day. They certainly never mentioned it to me, nor did I bring up the subject. His day of running away seems very tame by today's standards.

The documentary film, *Streetwise,* is about kids in Seattle who have run away. Most of the girls turn to prostitution and they turn to each other for help and support. They become each other's families. They live on the streets. Some of them survive, some of them don't. I first saw this film in New York and when it ended no one in the audience moved. We had all read about runaway kids. We knew the statistics. But getting to know these kids through this film was something else. What most of us were feeling, I think, was a sense of bewilderment. How could this be happening? Why aren't we doing anything to prevent it?

Dear Judy,

Listen, my name is Colette and I'm going into sixth grade. There's been a lot of stress in my family lately because of my sister. You see, my sister is sixteen and has been stealing. My parents knew about it but didn't want her to go to jail or to the Youth Detention Center so they never told.

Well, one day she told my parents she was sleeping over her friend's house and actually she ran away with her boyfriend, Gary. They were gone for five or six days. Then she came home with two burglary charges. My sister went to court in Somerville, and has to go again. She's still stealing, even now.

My dad got sick because of all this stress. He is better now and the family is doing okay. I really had to live through a lot. A lot of tears rolled down my pillow, believe me.

My dad and mom had so many arguments because of my sister. Now they don't. I'm not trying to get pity. What I want is someone to tell me, "You'll live through this." I thought you could be that person. Even a plain old letter would mean a lot to me.

Colette, age 11

3

A Mother's Story

Dear Judy,

I have a suggestion for a book for you. In millions of homes across this country teenage children are into drugs or stealing or other kinds of antisocial behavior. These emotionally disturbed children are living with older or younger siblings who have to cope with their parents' pain and preoccupation with the so-called "bad" child, not to mention their own feelings of anger and disappointment. It is a complicated business, one that our family is living through. I can't find the right words to help the other children release their feelings. I have read all your books as my nineteen- and sixteen-year-old daughters have, as well as my thirteen-year-old son.

Please consider this topic: How well-behaved children's lives are constantly being destroyed by these siblings. And there are so many of them in our small town.

Helen, adult

I encouraged Helen to write about her family and her feelings. She did, in the following letter.

Dear Judy,

As you know, I am a working mother with three in blue jeans and one in college. I've been trying to find the time to write down some of my observations for you. The point is to find a way to help all the siblings out there who have experienced a horror story such as ours.

Keith is now seventeen. At fourteen or fifteen he made some obscene phone calls. The police came. I promised to seek counseling for him. Keith would not go. Soon he refused to go to school and then he refused to do anything. The psychologist suggested that we sign some paper declaring him incorrigible and have him placed in a state home for a brief period of time.

We did, and Keith was there for four months. He learned to steal and deal drugs while he was there and when he came out he stole from everyone; my best friend, our neighbors, the family. He was heavily into drugs. Finally, we sent him to a special school for emotionally disturbed kids. Now he has been home since June. He seems to be doing well in private school and has some friends, but he is still into drugs.

The problem is not just Keith's or mine but the whole family's. Everyone is affected. Sara, nineteen, is glad to be away at college. She won't come home if she knows Keith will be here. Peggy, sixteen, is just a year and a half younger than Keith. She is not a good student but she is a super athlete, has lovely friends, is warm and tender but tries to hide it. She was close to Keith when they were young but his compulsive lying and hassling has made her very wary of him. When the trouble started she defended Keith. She would not believe any of it. My husband behaved in the same way. Now Peggy doesn't trust Keith at all. She always ends up hurt in some way when she plays a game with him or they have to share a chore. Consequently, I try to keep the chores separate but equal. Peggy puts Keith down all the time. She is deadly and she is accurate.

I think her anger is the most overwhelming force in her attitude toward him. Mine is a combination of love-guilt-anger-depression—sadness. In fact, I feel akin to mourning. But Peggy feels anger and doesn't understand the way Keith "gets away" with things and doesn't do "his share."

Philip is four years younger than Keith. He has a different personality. They both have the same supersensitivity to criticism. Keith strikes out but Philip cringes inward. Philip is naturally bright but he is not an athlete and is not at all competitive. He likes fashions, home decoration, working with colors and textures. He is the family sightseer, the traveler, the movie buff, the TV viewer. His friends are bright, nonathletes. They like shopping malls.

Philip hates Keith with a passion. Keith is physical and will grab Philip. Philip could kill him. He likes to see Keith punished or grounded. When the police came for Keith, Philip found it exciting.

My husband's heart broke a long time ago

along with the camera collection that Keith stole from him. He is a passive man and doesn't know what to do. He either strikes out or doesn't bother to do anything.

I've left out so much—changes of doctors, going to marriage counselors, family counselors. I wish you would write about the feelings of siblings going to psychologists because there are problems with one of their brothers or sisters, and their embarrassment about the whole thing. Philip actually thought that *he* was crazy.

I took off a morning to write this since working mothers rarely have quiet times in their houses. I hope you will want to write a book about these problems.

Helen, adult

Helen's story reminds me of a TV-movie called *Not My Kid*. It's about a fifteen-year-old girl, doing drugs. By the time her parents find out, her life is out of control. Her parents place her in a special school, which doubles as a treatment center for kids who are addicted to drugs or alcohol. Treatment involves the whole family, and at one session, for parents only, there is a poignant scene in which the girl's mother stands and says, "Sometimes I wish Susan wouldn't ever come home. Sometimes I wish Susan would just disappear." I think that's how many families feel when one child is a constant source of trouble. But as parents, we have responsibilities. We can't just give up on our kids. We have to try to find a way to help them.

4

Violence

Dear Judy,

My parents are divorced. My dad is an alcoholic. We used to only see him on weekends but now we don't see him at all because he was drunk the last time we went to see him. Mom divorced Dad because he beat her up and she found out he was an alcoholic. I go to Alateen. Mom goes to Al-Anon. My life is hard not having a dad, but I survive.

Robert, age 12

Family violence is often related to alcohol and it's a frightening subject. Kids don't know what to do about it. I don't know what to do when they write to me about it. I tried to find the child who wrote the following letter, but her address was vague and her phone number, which she included in her letter, had already been disconnected.

Dear Judy,

I am twelve years old. I'm not close with my mother at all. She's too busy going to discos. My father lives in the east with his future wife. Your books and thoughts express my personality.

My mother was arrested for child abuse. She beat me and my heart stopped. I need someone like you, a friend, a mother. I just can't believe my mother would do such a thing to me, of all people, but she was drunk. She drank a whole bottle of 151 proof rum. That's why! But still, she shouldn't drink in the first place, right? My father really hates me. He even told me so. He's a real jerk.

I love horses, cats, dogs and hamsters. I like John Travolta and Michael Jackson. Please send me a picture of your family and your house. I hope I live through this.

Alexandra, age 12

When Randy was a young teenager she had a friend, Maria, whose father was an alcoholic. Once, when Randy was invited to spend the night, Maria's father got drunk and her mother took the girls, who were already in their pajamas, to Maria's aunt's house, where they would be safe and not have to witness Maria's father's behavior. When Randy came home and told me what had happened, I wondered how Maria's mother was able to live that way and I understood why Maria was reluctant to bring her friends home.

Another teenager, Becky, fifteen, wrote to say that she suspects that her mother may be an alcoholic but she doesn't know what to do about it. Her parents are divorced. Becky has tried talking to her father about this but she feels guilty for telling on her mother instead of protecting her. Some days she feels that her mother is the child and she is the adult. Her mother isn't violent, but she sometimes passes out or can be forgetful and irresponsible. Her behavior frightens Becky.

Kids: I encouraged Becky to try to talk to her father again, even though she feels torn because of the divorce. I told her if she couldn't talk to him to confide in someone else. I also told her about Alateen (a group that helps the children of alcoholic parents) and Al-Anon (for friends or family of alcoholics). Their addresses are listed in the Resources section at the back of the book. If you are concerned that someone in your family has a drinking problem you can contact these groups yourself or ask someone to help you do it. Talking with others who have had the same problem can help, too.

Dear Judy,
   My family is horrible. They swear and they fight all the time. My brother doesn't know his own strength when he fights me. My father and my oldest brother fight with their bare hands over stupid things. When my sister and my father fight, my father drags her by the hair. I have told you this because you write about children and their problems. Do you have any suggestions for me?

Greta, age 10

Dear Judy,

I hope you write a book about someone like me so I can read it and find out who I am and where I belong. I don't have anyone to turn to. Once I got drunk and broke into a house and it was kind of fun. *No! I don't want to think that.*

I hate my sister, I really do. She hits me every time she doesn't get her way! My mom doesn't understand and she doesn't have time to listen. My father isn't the type and I don't want to talk to him anyway. My brother, now there's someone who I could talk to. But my parents kicked him out of the house. I'll never forgive them for that. I loved him so much. I don't even know if he's alive anymore.

When I grow up I'm going to write books like yours and I hope my mom reads them.

Shannon, age 14

Dear Judy,

Hi, my name is Lindsay. I'm in fifth grade. I was wondering if you could give me some advice. My parents are divorced and I live with my mom and stepdad. He owns a lumberyard and me, my mom, my brother and my stepdad run it. I go to my real dad's house every three weekends. He is also remarried and has two stepkids.

My stepdad's name is Neal. Neal always yells at me. I admit that I have a smart mouth but he hits me for nothing, sometimes. One time their friends were coming over on Saturday night. One couple had little kids and I was going to baby-sit them and I was asking my mom for about the third time if they were going to come soon, and

234

that's when Neal said, "It's time to go to bed, Lindsay." I said, "Well, I was going to baby-sit." He said, "Go to bed right now!"

So I went to my room and thought about it. And then I went out into the hall and I called to my mom and Neal said, "What do you want, Lindsay?" I said, "I wasn't talking to you." He said something but I couldn't hear him because of the air conditioner. Then he got up from his chair and I ran back to my room and he came in and he said, "All right, Lindsay," and he got me and whipped me with his hand and I fell off the bed and he elbowed me in the back and he got his belt and I got up and he whipped me and I fell across the other side of the bed and he came over where I was and he started to whip me again but I scooted across the other side and I was closing my eyes and didn't see him come over and he whipped me again and I screamed for my mom and my hand got in the way and he whipped me on the arm and I had the mark on my arm for about one week.

I talked to my mom but she didn't believe me. So I said, "Well, if you're not going to do anything about it I'll call the Child Abuse number." She said, "You do and I'll whip you!"

I was wondering what I should do? I was thinking that I could move in with my dad when I'm in seventh grade. But I'm not sure.

Lindsay, age 11

I wrote back to Lindsay advising her to confide in someone she could trust—either her father or a teacher at school or a counselor. If that didn't work, I told her to go ahead and call the Child Abuse number. She wrote back:

Dear Judy,

I got your letter. Sorry I wrote so late. I was in Florida for two weeks. I just got back. I was visiting my cousins, my aunts and uncles and my grandma. My grandma feels sorry for me.

I thought about what you said, but I really don't have anyone to talk to about it, anyone that cares. My mom just sticks up for Neal. My sister, who lives with my dad, doesn't like my mother very much. She wants me to come live with my dad, too, but I really don't want to because I'll miss my mom too much. Even though I don't feel right living with Neal. I think he's going to try something, if you know what I mean.

My life is mixed up and I don't know what to do. I thought about talking to the social worker. My sister said she overheard my dad and my stepmom talking about my mom. My dad said that the money he sends every month, for me and my brother, my mom just spends on the lumberyard and that's all she really cares about.

I'm just shaking right now. What should I do?

Lindsay, age 11

I wrote back but I never heard from Lindsay again. I hope that she's okay. I hope that she did talk with a social worker or her father and that she's safe and living with adults who care about her. We're all so anxious to stay out of each other's family business that sometimes we choose to ignore the signs of real trouble. Some states have laws requiring that suspected cases of child abuse be reported to the authorities. If you have reason to believe that a child is being abused, pick up the phone and make that call, whether or not you live in such a state. At the time that Lindsay wrote I didn't call the authorities. That was a mistake.

5

Rape

Dear Judy,

Hi! My name is Tammy and I wrote to you once before. I thought I'd write you again because I thought maybe you could write a book or story on rape. You write so good and you have not yet written on rape. You see, my sister, Vanessa, got raped and so I know everything about it. She went to trial but the guy won. He was sixty-five years old and she was only fifteen. I know him. He lives near here and it's real scary having him live so close. The incident happened six months ago. I was at the trial.

Rape is such a common crime nowadays. My sister told me all about it. Me and Vanessa are more friends than sisters. We're really close. She tells me everything and I tell her everything. I think we know each other better than our mom does. We can speak without talking, if you know what I mean, and we always know how the other is feeling.

I can remember some things about the incident that Vanessa doesn't, because she's blocked some of it out. She went through a terrible time. It just about tore me up inside, watching her. I can just imagine how hard it was for her.

I'm writing not to get attention but because I care. I think people ought to realize how much the rape victim and her family goes through. It puts stress on everyone.

Tammy, age 13

The letters in this chapter are very painful to read. They deal with experiences that most of us have never had and pray we never will. The anguish that I feel when I read letters like these leaves me in despair. There is so little that I can actually do. But we can't deny that some kids are living in situations that are intolerable and experiencing events that will leave permanent scars.

In the following section, which is about incest, one of the mothers of an incest victim said she knew, deep inside, that something was very wrong in her family. She suspected, but she could not deal with the implications, and so, for a long time, she pretended it was not happening. But it is happening, in every community and in every economic group. We have to face it and educate our kids, so that they understand what is okay and what is not.

6

Incest

Dear Judy,
   I like your books because they come to life
when you read them. The main reason I'm writing
to you is because I would like to see a book
written about a problem a few kids have. I'm
twelve years old and my two sisters and I are
incest victims.
   In most of your other books you write about
how kids feel and their emotions on different
situations. My question is, could you possibly
write a book on incest from a kid's point of view?
It would help them understand their feelings and
emotions.
   My mother and I would be glad to tell you our
story.

Carrie, age 12

Carrie and I corresponded for about a year before
the TV-movie *Something About Amelia* was first

shown. Carrie wrote the following letter after she had seen it.

Dear Judy,

The reason I am writing so late at night is because I just finished watching *Something About Amelia,* a TV-movie about incest. I don't know if you had a chance to watch it or not.

It was mainly true, with lots of feelings and crying. Now it's been three years for us, the week before my tenth birthday, in fact. I had to go and make my statement on my birthday! Anyway, three years is a long time and it's mainly forgotten. My two other sisters don't even talk to our father but I go up and visit sometimes.

My brother and my mom, me and my sisters, talk a lot about it. I'm glad that I'm able to write to you because I haven't told any friends except I have one very close friend I may tell soon because it won't change anything between us. She is very understanding.

My aunt and uncles and my mom's mom and dad know. And my aunt sat down with her eight-year-old daughter and watched that movie tonight and explained it to her. My uncles are very supportive too. Me and my sisters are very lucky because we have supportive relatives and a mom who really cares. She is a neat lady. She worked at a place called We-Care where people answered the phones and helped other people with their problems. She also went on the local noon news to make people more aware that this (incest) is happening. (She was silhouetted.) She and two friends formed a Mothers of

Incested Children group. They wrote an article about it.

Carrie, age 13

Dear Judy,

The reason I am writing you is because my life would make a perfect story. I'm not asking you to write a book on my life. I'm just giving you some ideas for your use. I'll start from the beginning.

1970: This was the year I was born. I was born in an Atlanta hospital. My mom never knew that my father was already married and had a family somewhere else until after she got pregnant. She called around and that's how she found out but she never saw him again. After I was born she decided to keep working in Atlanta so she flew me to Idaho where my relatives all lived and left me with them until I was one year old.

Then she got married to a man named Wally. He was an insurance agent. We moved into a new house in Twin Falls, Idaho. And one year later my brother Tom was born. Two years after Tom was born my sister, Abigail, was born and we were each two years apart. When I was six we moved to Boise, Idaho, for about half a year. Out of all the houses we have ever lived in this one was my favorite.

Before I go any further I would like to explain something that was happening that changed my life in a big way.

My stepfather, Wally, had been molesting me since I was five years old. When I was that little I thought all dads were supposed to do that so I didn't tell anyone. We soon moved again, in Boise, six months later. We only stayed in that house for another six months. This time we moved north. It was a *lot* different here. There were rattlesnakes and cows, horses, and all sorts of animals. Me and my brother and sister liked it a lot. Things between me and my stepdad went on pretty much as they always had with one small difference. Now I knew that what he did was wrong.

My mom worked so she never caught him. The reason I never told Mom or anyone else was because I was afraid my stepdad would kill my mom. This all went on until I was nine-and-a-half years old.

Then one morning my mom caught him with me and it was out. He went to work as usual and mom called the police to report this. That same afternoon I had some tests taken to see if I was pregnant. After it was done and the tests were negative we packed up the camper and went to my relatives to live with them for a while.

1980: We were now living with my grandparents. All of my relatives knew about what had happened. For five years he molested me, sometimes daily, and it was finally *over*. Wally's sister, Audrey, lived next door to my Aunt Evelyn and she blamed it all on me. Because by now Wally was in the State Institute. We lived in a small farming community. The town was so small that practically everyone was related in some way. Audrey made it known through the town that somehow it was my fault that her brother was in a mental institute.

Evelyn, my aunt, was Audrey's best friend, and

she started believing that Wally was in the right. One Christmas I can really remember she made us call him and ask how he was. (He was now out of the institution and living on a farm.) He sent us Christmas presents and birthday money. My brother and sister never understood why we didn't like him because they were still pretty young.

But now I had a new problem. I had a urinary-tract infection and it caused me to wet the bed and my pants. I had this since I was five and it was caused by Wally and what he did to me. Mom, Abigail, Tom and me all moved to an apartment in a town which was about ten miles from where Audrey and Evelyn lived. I started fifth grade there.

Every class has one person they pick on *all* of the time. And I happened to become that person, mainly because of my wetting problem. This lasted into the sixth grade when I had my appendix removed. Something happened then and I no longer had my problem. But the kids in my class never stopped teasing. Fifth grade was so bad that I would go home crying after school. Or I would tell the principal I was sick.

Well, when I got done with the eighth grade I went into high school. My freshman year was the best year of school I had ever known. In my area all the little schools go to one big high school so there were a lot of kids who didn't know about my previous problem. Soon I was one of the most popular kids in my class and believe me I *worked* for it! I was not good-looking (just average) but I had put myself high up because I had a good personality. I was the wild type. The reason I wasn't the most popular in my class was because I made friends with *everyone,* including the squares. I guess I'm the type who is always looking for more and more people to have fun with.

At my first homecoming dance I met Vince and we started to date. I was the first person in the class to date and everyone was totally shocked that it was me! Soon we went steady and this went on for *seven months.* The last four months I hated. I wanted to say no, but I couldn't get him to break up with me without hurting him. But I finally did.

During my high school and grade school years I tried to commit suicide about fifteen times. Since eighth grade I've been seeing a psychiatrist and still am. She's helped a lot. But my mother doesn't think I need to see her anymore. My life has been some mess! I can't help feeling that if it weren't for Wally I wouldn't have half of these problems. I would kill him if I ever saw him!

My mom got married again but he didn't adopt me or my brother and sister so we still have Wally's last name. My mom had a baby boy, Christopher, with my new stepfather and now she is pregnant again. My new stepfather is an okay person.

Lately I've been considering suicide again. In a drawer in my room I have everything I would ever need. Razor blades, knives, pills and other stuff. The funny thing is I really don't want to kill myself. I want to go to acting school and become famous. But my main goal in life is to find my *real* father. I may need help with that but I *will* find him.

Please write me a letter. I know you get hundreds of letters but please help me through this.

Forever a Fan . . .

Suzanne, age 16

I wrote, urging Suzanne to yell for help if those feelings surface again. "Call anyone," I told her. "Call your psychiatrist, call a hot-line number, but don't wait!" We continue to correspond and I hope she'll be okay.

Dear Judy,

I am a physician and I am writing to ask if you would consider approaching the problem of child sexual abuse in one of your books.

Children need a source of comfort for their pain, memories, scary secrets. They desperately need a book which says it's okay to say no to a grown-up. That if something confusing happens they should tell a trusted grown-up right away. And when something *very* bad happens between a grown-up and a child, it is the grown-up who is responsible. The child is always blameless. They need a book that says, "You are not dirty or bad or ugly. Pretending it didn't happen doesn't make it go away. There is help out there. There are people who care. Don't give up. Someone loves you. There are rules and laws that protect you and won't let the grown-up person hurt you. None of it is your fault."

In order to prevent sexual and physical abuse, we need books that will inform children, letting them know that they have the right to ask for help if they need it.

I have been continually surprised to realize that the majority of my patients have a single incident or, more often, a long period of abuse in their histories. The ongoing pain is incalculable. It forms the unstable foundation for the development of the self-concept, the future parent, community leader, person.

As a parent, as well as a physician, I feel that we need a way to protect tomorrow's and today's children. And we need a way to soften the pain for yesterday's children. Please consider the topic.

Harriet, adult

7

Tracy's Story

Dear Judy,

I'm twelve, going on thirteen. I have two younger sisters and an older brother but he doesn't live with us. He took off more than a year ago. I live in Sacramento. I don't like it here as much as where I used to live. I've been here for almost two-and-a-half years now. I still have hardly any friends and no close friends that I can talk to. I really need someone to talk to about things that have happened. I want to ask my parents some questions about my brother but I don't know when or how to.

Please write me at least a short letter.

Love,
Tracy, age 12

Dear Judy,

Last night was one of those nights. I just couldn't fall asleep. I've been thinking about my brother, Dennis, a lot lately. I wrote you before and told you I had questions to ask my family. Well, I'm afraid to ask them, because they might break down and cry which would maybe make me feel guilty. I hate it when people ask me about Dennis. One time I really lost my temper at someone who asked where my brother was and I yelled, almost crying, "Why do you ask me so many questions . . . why can't you just shut up?" She looked at me with hurt in her eyes and on her face. She said, "I'm sorry, I didn't mean to hurt you. I really am sorry." Then she took me into her arms and just let me cry. It was the first time I had cried, ever since Dennis left home. I didn't think I needed to cry. I guess I did though.

Well, I'll let you go now. You're probably busy.

Love,
Tracy, age 12

Dear Judy,

I'm going to tell you something that only four, maybe five, people in the whole world know (outside our family). He, my brother Dennis, well, to put it plainly, I was a victim of incest for seven years. Seven gruesome horrifying years of unwanted sexual harassment from him. But the last time we ever had sexual contact, more than a year ago, I told him that I was going back to San Diego, to live with my grandma. I had been thinking of doing that to get away from Dennis but I didn't know how to tell my parents. Two days later Dennis took off. I figured that he left because he wouldn't be able to harass me any-more.

I never liked the incest. It was my body. I always dreaded when he'd make me touch him and I had to let him touch me. I just hated it. It's a relief now that he's gone away. I'm glad the sex is over. That left a huge emotional scar, should I say, actually, a still open wound. I have to go now. Write me when you have time. What do you think about all of the things I've just told you?

Love you always,
Tracy, age 13

Dear Judy,
  No, I don't have anyone to talk with about it (the incest). Well, actually, I have told one or two people just to get it off my shoulders. They're willing to talk about it but I'm too embarrassed, scared and guilty about it to say much.
  My parents do know about it, but they sure don't act like it. They've never really tried to help me, they've just buried it and acted as though nothing had ever happened. It had though, for seven years. They seem to expect me to act as though nothing ever happened, like nothing hurts inside. But it does. It hurts a lot.

Tracy, age 13

Dear Judy,
  I saw *Something About Amelia*, the TV movie about incest, but only about a total of fifteen minutes of it. Mom was home so every time she left the room I turned it to the movie and turned it back when I heard her coming back. I asked a

teacher about it after school and she gave me a complete summary of the movie in about fifteen minutes. At least it only happened to Amelia for two years, while I had to suffer for seven years. And at least her mom finally accepted it. My mom sure never did. She never even did anything to stop it. It's like she didn't care. She got off the hook and never had to face up to it. Now I have to.

Hey, I told a teacher of mine about what happened and I just started seeing a professional counselor. (Thanks anyway for offering to try to find me someone here.)

Lots of love,
Tracy, age 13

Dear Judy,

I stopped seeing my counselor. Summer is near and I couldn't see her over the summer. I've sorted out tons of feelings about the incest and I'm just about convinced that it wasn't my fault. I sure wish I could tell Dennis how shitty he's made my life, how much pain he's put me through and how many scars he's left. I wish he could get into trouble for what he did. He did it, then just left me with all the guilt, embarrassment and anger and made me deal with it all, sort out my shattered life, piece back together my existence. I'm glad though that he told someone the day before he left, what happened between us. So then I didn't have to keep it bottled up inside.

Love lots,
Tracy, age 13

Dear Judy,

I have just gotten back from a two-and-a-half-week vacation with my parents and sisters. I suppose I really changed your perspective on the matter when I told you that Dennis had told someone about what happened. He told a counselor who had really *forced* it out of him. I found out that he didn't tell all, just that it had happened. Naturally the family blamed me, telling me that I *let* him do it. But how the hell was I supposed to stop it? Sure I told him no. I knew it wasn't right to do what he was doing to me. Besides, it hurt like crazy a lot of the time. He was so big and I was so small. I'll never forget how it felt, never forget what he did to me and how much he screwed up my life.

How could he do that to me? *Why* did he do it? I never wanted him to, I never told him to, I hate him! I *really* hate him. So he goes ahead and takes off. Everyone says how much they miss their little angel. They all cried when he left home. But there was one person who didn't cry. She was angry. Angry that he left her with all the blame, all the guilt, all the shit that people gave her. That person is me. An attractive girl, a kind girl, a girl who treasures her friends and one who rarely swears unless she's very, very angry. And I am angry! Everyone blames it on me. Everyone except you, my closest friends and a counselor who I can't talk to.

I think that way down deep inside I still believe that I was to blame. I can say that I know it wasn't my fault, people can tell me it wasn't my fault, but way down deep, I think I still feel a twinge of guilt. That will be there the rest of my life.

This is the year. The incest started ten years ago. Can you imagine . . . it began when I was four and he was twelve. My sister, Lisa, was born the same year. My feelings are intense, deep, heartbreaking and very, very painful. I'm going to talk about it someday. Until then, I bury my feelings deeper inside. And I cry myself to sleep many nights.

I hope to meet you someday. Until that time you are in my thoughts. I send you joy and peace.

I love you.
Tracy, age 14

Dear Judy,

Sometimes I wonder if you would forget me if I didn't write to you for a long time. It's been many months since I've written and I'm sorry. A lot of things have happened since the last time I wrote. Main things include trying out for a one-act play, making it and doing lots of performances.

Oh, I joined a group of teenaged girls who were all victims of incest. It's like a group therapy thing. Last week concluded an eight-week segment. Yesterday we began our next segment. Those eight weeks were good for me. I got a chance to talk about my feelings and was comforted. I realized how much I needed good therapy.

Still, I'm feeling so confused tonight. Tomorrow it will be three years since Dennis left home. I don't even know if he's dead or alive. It's so tense it hurts. I feel so alienated when all my confused feelings surface. I'm *expected* to miss him. But how can I miss him?

Love,
Tracy, age 14

Tracy, like Carrie and Suzanne, shared her story because writing about her very painful experiences helped her to sort out some of her feelings. All three of them want to let others know it can happen and that children do not always know what to do about it.

In educating kids about sexual abuse, we want to stress awareness, not fear. We want to give them confidence so that if they are approached they will know what to say and what to do. We want them to learn to be strong and to feel in control of their own bodies, so that they will never be afraid to say no, so that they cannot be intimidated or threatened by family, friends or relatives, any more than by strangers.

Kids: If someone is harassing you or forcing you to have sex, confide in an adult you can trust—a teacher, a counselor, someone in the family, a grown-up friend. Don't wait! Help is available. Look in the Resources section at the end of this book to find agencies you can contact. And remember, incest is never the fault of the victimized child.

Chapter X
OUT OF CONTROL

1

Depression

Dear Judy,
I have only one question for you. I've really
been depressed lately and, well, do a lot of teens
think seriously about suicide? Because I do a lot. I
was wondering if a lot of teens really consider it.

Noreen, age 16

Sometimes, if I am feeling down, especially at night, I
tell myself that it will all seem brighter tomorrow
morning. Tomorrow morning my cereal will be waiting,
the sky might be blue, another day means another
beginning. But I can't make others feel the same way. I
wish I could help every young person who feels depressed. All I can do is give my support and hope that
they will find their way back, that they will find that
reason to live.

I'm not qualified to discuss depression from a medi-
cal viewpoint. What I know firsthand is that we all have

our ups and downs. The will to live is strong, and if you have a reason for facing another day, you do. There is a difference between feeling low and serious depression. The letters in this section are about that difference.

Dear Judy,

I really don't know how to put it! But I do need your help. I'm fourteen and I really like these boys named Matt and Steve. Well, Matt moved and I found out that he only used me (in *that* kind of way) and so did Steve. Now I think no one likes me. I will never get a boyfriend. I think I am ugly.

I can't go to my mother or father because my father doesn't even love me and my mother is very hard to talk to. When I try to talk to her she doesn't even want to listen.

I can't take the pressure anymore. I don't know what to do! Please, do you have any advice? I don't even go to school anymore because I'm always down. I don't even want to get out of bed.

Please help!

Kay, age 14

Dear Judy,

Hi! My name is Brenda. I wrote to you a while ago. I said I was depressed and thought of suicide. You said that if I couldn't get rid of these feelings I should get professional help.

After I wrote you I kept sinking lower and lower. One night I took twenty-two aspirin. I slept quite a bit but aside from that nothing happened. As I lay in bed the next morning I remembered your letter.

I am now going to a psychiatrist. I'm feeling much better. Since January no suicidal thoughts have entered my mind. My problems are a long way from being solved but I feel better.

Brenda, age 15

Dear Judy,

I am a fifteen-year-old girl. I've had a very disturbing childhood and now I can finally tell people about it. Besides family and doctors you are the only person I've ever told this to. You seem to understand teenagers so much that I figure you'd understand my problems, which nobody, not even my parents, understand.

Between the ages of eight and fourteen I had a drinking problem, I smoked, my friends got busted for pot and drugs (I never touched pot and drugs though). My very best friend, Jennifer, got pregnant and just had a baby girl. My boyfriend Todd (of ten months) broke up with me and because of that I went into a deep depression and was sent to a mental clinic. I was extremely obese and terribly ugly. I was put under supervision because I tried suicide.

A year ago I went into therapy and now I'm cured of most of my problems. Now, you might say to yourself, Why is she telling this to me? Because I think problems like these should be put into books so that teenagers can read them. I wanted desperately to write a book on the experiences I went through. I was hoping if I told you about them you might decide to write a book on one of these past experiences.

Just one more thing. Lots of people (strangers) think I'd be a bad influence on them or their kids. It hurts a lot. I've been called a lot of things by total strangers and I hope you don't think I'm less of a person or that all my problems make me a bad person. (I'm really sure you wouldn't though.)

I'm deeply interested in helping other teenagers who are like what I used to be. Thank you for taking the time to read my letter.

Alisa, age 15

Dear Judy,

In April of 1984 my grandmother Elsa died of internal failure. At the age of thirteen I almost died, too. I was a wreck for the next few months but began to hide my feelings and become moody. In my room I cried. The crying lasted almost a year then . . .

On March 10, 1985, I jumped out my window hoping the end of my suffering was in sight. I was put into a hospital. There I talked with kids with the same problems. I was released a month later.

One afternoon in May, while browsing in a bookstore I saw your book *Tiger Eyes*. I picked up the book and started to read. Judy, your book has taught me . . . *there are so many memories . . . but you can't go back. Not ever. You have to pick up the pieces and keep moving on . . .*

Thank you for all your help.

Nicholas, age 14

Dear Judy,

My name is Molly. I have maybe a suggestion on what you could write a book on, that affects many kids my age, (sixteen). What it's like to be very depressed for a few years and how it feels, what it's like to attempt suicide, have thoughts on running away and trying it and getting caught. How it feels when you're absolutely crying on the inside and you can feel it too. When you're screaming for help on the inside and nobody can hear you until it's almost too late and all the damage is done. *Finally* when you do get help, even if it means having to go into a hospital for a few months, what it's like to finally become aware of who you are, what it's like to come seeping out of a shell you built around yourself. Also, the effects it has on the rest of the family.

I really think this kind of a book would appeal to teenagers because I know friends of mine have thought about suicide and are *very* curious to know how it feels (even if it's a feeble attempt) and all your thoughts behind it. I also think that kids would like to read about someone who's depressed. Then maybe they could see what's normal depression and what isn't. Maybe you could write about a teen in a hospital and how they learn to be able to handle reality. What it's like to become very close to people in the hospital and one day have to say goodbye and what a therapeutic community is really like.

I'd really like to hear your opinions on some of these ideas on books and if you do maybe decide to write a book on one of these suggestions and you need to find out what it's like to go through all of this and how it feels and all the emotions behind it, you can talk to me, because I've been through everything I've written and more.

Thanks.

Molly, age 16

When I experienced mild depression, following my divorce, I felt that there was no one I could turn to—no real friends to confide in, no family to listen without judging, no one who really understood or cared. I think that's how most of these kids feel—completely alone and alienated, often without hope.

If you are a parent, take your child's feelings seriously. Too often we don't want to acknowledge the signs that something is wrong. We go along hoping that the problem will miraculously disappear. Some parents would rather bury their heads in the sand than take action. The kinds of problems kids are writing about in this chapter may be more than the family can handle themselves. It can be a relief to finally admit, "Yes, we have a problem." Because only then can you get help and begin to solve it.

2

Drugs

Dear Judy,
  If you ever wrote a book on *Should I Smoke Pot?* it would be a bestseller.

Eddie, age 17

While I've tried to remain nonjudgmental with the characters in my books and I don't tell the kids who write to me what to do or not to do, I have very negative feelings about the use of drugs and alcohol. I have never seen one good thing come of it.

Larry's high school class (1981) was a drug-oriented group. He went to a small school in New Mexico, with under forty kids in each class, and I saw too many of them lost, burned-out and wasted. Why were drugs necessary for these kids? "Drugs make you more creative and better able to cope. Drugs help you learn more about yourself, drugs expand your mind, drugs help you to relax . . ." were some of the answers.

I asked them to tell me *how* drugs made them more creative, *how* drugs helped them cope with the world. And not one kid was able to present a strong case, was able to make me say, "Oh, yeah . . . I see what you mean." Instead, what I saw were kids who used drugs and alcohol as an excuse—as a way of not having to learn to cope with reality, of not having to learn how to handle their own lives, or how to handle responsibility, disappointments, stress, rejection and even pleasure. I saw drugs and alcohol used as an excuse for not having to confront those feelings that are buried deep inside.

Kids: If drugs or alcohol become the focal point of your life ask yourself why. Write down your reasons. Then think about them. If I ever wrote the book that Eddie asked me to in his letter it would be really short. It would say, "Don't do it!"

Dear Judy,
  What I would like to see in a future book is an eighth or ninth grader dealing with pressures of peers trying to get him or her to try pot or other drugs. Grass is a buck a joint and strong tranquilizers are the same in the hallways at my school. A fourteen-year-old girl OD'd at school last year.
  I smoked for two months: I am not proud of that fact but I know most kids go from cigs to grass to pills (uppers and downers) to sometimes having to shoot up every morning to get going. I sincerely hope one of your future books is about drugs, their use and how kids get pressured into using them and the consequences. If you don't write about it I will.

Jamie, age 13

264

Dear Judy,

I am a girl, thirteen years old. I feel that I can tell you my problems because I can't tell my mom. Not now, because it's too late and I've gone too far.

Last year I was a happy seventh grader. I got the best grades of my class and got along with all my teachers and was very popular. Then, last summer, my grandma died. We were very, very close. After that everything just fell apart. I just couldn't handle it. I slept in my parents' bedroom for a month because I was so afraid at night. I thought my grandma was going to haunt me. That's how mixed up I was. I tried to talk to my father but he couldn't understand. I used to have horrible nightmares.

Then one night I was baby-sitting for my neighbors. It was July so I stayed and rapped a little. They were both burnouts and dopers. They sold pot, coke, hashish and Quaaludes in large quantities. Well, anyway, they asked me if I wanted to smoke a joint. I said fine. They smoked a couple of doobies with me and by the time I went home I was loaded.

Anyway, that night I had a great dream and I wasn't scared. So I started smoking pot. I baby-sat for my neighbors and they paid me in pot instead of cash. This was over the summer. By the time school started again I was a burnout. I started getting in fights with my teachers and I ended up in the office three days out of five. On my final report card I had seven unacceptables. I still passed because they wanted to get rid of me.

I don't have the problem about death much anymore but now I have a much bigger problem. Over the school year I got into harder stuff. Now I

snort cocaine and take speed every now and then.
I smoke pot about three times a day. I even tried
acid once but after I did a friend of mine went
crazy when he was on it and killed himself so I
never tried it again. But now I just don't know
how to get off the stuff.

Maybe you should write a book about drugs. It
would help. I would greatly appreciate advice
because I need some bad. Anyway, thanks for
your time even though I'm not sure I'm worth it.

Beverly, age 13

Problems with drugs and alcohol cross all lines and
all ages. I heard from the youngest child of a well-to-do
family, living in the suburbs. His older brothers are
both in their early twenties and are very straight. But
he is a rebel. He has been experimenting with drugs
since junior high school. He is bright and creative, but
his values conflict with his parents'. He is struggling to
be different from the rest of his family. He feels that
their expectations are suffocating him and that he will
never fit into the family mold. His parents are concerned, and with good reason. What will become of
him?

His method of breaking away is not one I would
encourage but I hope his parents remain willing to sit
down and talk with him, listening to his side as carefully
as they want him to listen to theirs. I hope they
continue to let him know how much they care about
him and believe in him. If they can recognize his
differences without judging him, if they can allow him
the freedom to grow in his own way, I think he will be
okay.

Katrin, on the other hand, is more self-destructive.

She is from a very wealthy family. She has felt alone and alienated for years. She uses money from her trust fund to support her cocaine addiction. I don't know if she will find her way back or not.

I know a man in his forties who has never grown up. Smoking dope and dropping acid is as important to him today as it was when he was a hippie in the sixties. I don't like being with him. I don't find stoned people interesting or amusing. And I sympathize with his kids, who are teenagers. They don't find him amusing either.

A friend calls me a fanatic on the subject of drugs. That's okay with me. I'd rather tell kids my true feelings than put on some act in order to gain their favor.

3

Laura's Story

Laura lives in a small factory town in Maine. She is the youngest, by more than a dozen years, of nine children. She has shiny, waist-length black hair, blue eyes and pale skin. I know because I have a photo of her, holding a tabby cat. It is a photo that I look at often.

I never dreamed I would become so emotionally involved with Laura. But I have. In the three years we have been exchanging letters Laura has painted a picture of her life. She has drawn characters so vividly I feel that I know them. She is a natural and a gifted writer. None of her teachers know this and her family doesn't either. She floats along in school.

Laura has written about many subjects, but I think she has written as honestly as anyone ever has about drugs and a life that is getting out of control. The following are excerpts from her letters.

Dear Judy,
    Hi! I'm a fourteen-year-old book junkie and I hope to be a famous author someday. In all your

books I could find a part of myself, either now or when I was younger. But I've been wondering if you've realized how much times have changed.

Hardly anyone I know is a virgin. I know a lot of kids just say things like that to impress their friends but I also know it can be true.

I could tell you some stories that would pop your eyeballs out of their sockets, but I won't. You probably wouldn't understand or relate to some of the things I've been through, such as smoking pot since the age of ten.

I'll keep reading your books, hoping to find something by you about some *real* problems.

See ya!

Love from a fan,
Laura, age 14

Dear Judy,

Hi! I was surprised to get an answer from you. My own sisters only write to me about once a month. I haven't seen any of them for about a year. I found it hard to believe that you actually *listen* to your kids. If I suggested to *my* parents to listen to me they'd probably have my head checked. My dad told me he never did want me and that if it were his choice I wouldn't be born. They already had their family when I came along. My mom wanted me but she doesn't trust me at all. I'm an outsider in my own home.

My cousin, Rose, who's sixteen, snorts cocaine often and says it's the greatest. My other cousin, Paulette, who's thirteen, tells me not to play games with my life. My brother drinks liquor and always tells me to drink some. My best friend tells me to stay away from liquor.

I have no sense of what's wrong and what's right anymore. Different people tell me different things. I guess I'll go now, Judy. Thank you for writing to me.

Laura, age 14

Dear Judy,

A lot has happened to me since I last wrote. I've fallen in love with an older man. He's one of my brother's friends and is twenty-seven. His name is Jimmy. He's not like my brother's other friends, who get drunk all the time and are loud and rowdy and haven't any manners. He's sweet and nice and considerate.

Every single person I love is on something. Annie, my best friend, is on pot, so is Jimmy, the man I've fallen for, and my sisters, too. It's impossible to sit around listening to people talk about being high constantly and not want to do it yourself. Or to sit in a room and watch other people smoke pot and get high and not want to smoke when they hand it to you.

Well, I guess I'll go now. You're a special friend, too.

Laura, age 14

Dear Judy,

So much has changed since I last wrote you a letter. Not family situations—they're the same. It's me. I'm smoking pot regularly again. I'm doing worse in school. I drink, cuss, lie, cheat and steal. Should I go on? I hate cops, school and myself, among other things. Well, not really myself. I don't hate the person inside, not the *real* me. I just hate how I must appear to everyone else. How I act, the things I say and do.

Oh, that man I mentioned . . . Jimmy . . . well, I love him. I really do. He says he cares about me, but that it's hard to care about someone who doesn't really seem to care about herself. He claims he wouldn't even smoke pot if I didn't.

I'm all confused now. What's happening to everyone? What's the difference between right and wrong? It seems like no one knows or cares anymore. Right now I'm feeling bad and don't feel like telling about anything else at this time.

Please write and tell me what you think.

Laura, age 14

Dear Judy,

This is me again, Laura. I know that I have to quit smoking pot. Listen, Judy, for a while Jimmy and I quit smoking during the week. We just smoked it during the weekend. Guess what happened then? My attendance at school improved a lot. I brought my math grade up from a D to an A+. Because Jimmy helped me understand it and because he cared enough to encourage me to stop smoking. Before that I'd thought about quitting school. But I didn't. He talked me out of it and I'm glad. I love Jimmy more than anyone in the world and I'd do anything for him because I know he wouldn't want me to do anything bad for myself or anyone else. He's straightened me out a lot. I used to rip off everything—pot, makeup, cigarettes, anything. Now I don't. I missed twenty-nine days the first few months of school. Since then, none.

Laura, age 14

Dear Judy,

Jimmy and I started smoking pot again during the week. But we've decided together that we have to quit. Jimmy said he doesn't think I can. He thinks I'm hooked. I might be. It takes a lot more pot to make me high now than it used to. Lots more.

Yes, I've heard before, too, that girls who fall in love with older men are really wanting father figures. I've also heard that older men who like younger girls are insecure. Jimmy wishes I were a lot older, or he was a lot younger but no one can change our age difference. Or the way we feel. So we say to hell with what everyone else thinks.

I really, truly want to be a writer. The money wouldn't be bad, a lot more than I'd make working in the factory or hamburger stand, like most of the people around here. All they ever do is complain about not making enough money. I don't want to end up like that. That's not the only reason I want to write though. I find enjoyment in it when I'm straight. I won't be able to smoke pot and get all fogged up and out of it if I try to write seriously. Anyway, I'm so shy. Really, I am! I get embarrassed real easy. When I write, though, it's different. I can communicate and express myself better on paper than with words.

I need to stay busy. That's the only way to quit smoking pot. To stay occupied, so you won't think about it so much, mostly when you have a lot of free time. Because when you're a heavy pot smoker, as soon as you're bored, your mind is on pot.

I'm trying to get a job or something. To occupy time, plus buy what I need, at least—clothes and makeup and diet pills and Visine and magazines and books. It's a big hassle though. No one wants to hire a fourteen-year-old. And even if somebody would hire me I'd have no way of getting to the job.

You wouldn't believe how much money poor people spend on dope. It's unrealistic and incredible. Dope is the main reason most of the jerks around here don't have *anything* by the time they're forty. Really. Because . . . like I said, they spend every cent on dope. I know. I've been around long enough. It's kind of pitiful and sad to see people nod and scratch and not *know* what's going on anywhere around them.

I'll go for now. I hope to hear from you sometime soon.

Laura, age 14

Dear Judy,
Life is so strange. I don't know what I want. When I'm sober and straight I have so many goals. What I want most in the world is to be a success and to make a good comfortable living. But when I'm doped up, dreams or goals are unrealistic. Any kind of a goal. The life of a pothead is so much different than a straight.

Yes, Judy, I tried to quit smoking pot with Jimmy just as we'd planned. It didn't work out though. As usual. It never does. We always plan to quit and within a week one of us has backed out and broke his or her word. It always goes that way. Always. Just as I start to get used to the idea of getting on with my future, and my life, I mess it up. Either Jimmy forgets and smokes some reefer or I do. Usually him. He said he'd quit with me, though, anytime. During the week, for months at a time, or even permanently. The problem is that I can't decide. When I'm high, I say, "To hell with school, piss on education and I don't need anything from society." Those thoughts aren't true though. Not to the real world. When you're high, it doesn't matter. When you're high, you think exactly how you wish to think.

Smoking dope regularly will give you headaches, stomachaches, make you vomit . . . depending on the individual. It gets to where you can't think clearly. It's difficult to pay attention to things, extremely easy to forget things. It's like you're in a deep fog all the time. In a daze.

You know, when I was younger I used to sniff glue—rubber cement. I'm lucky someone (Jimmy) cared enough to make me quit before I hadn't any brain cells left. That stuff will make you *trip*. It'll put you into your own spooky, paranoid, solitary, frightening little world where everything is carefree and simple and beautiful. You hear noises in your ears and you see the edges of your vision blur and sort of vibrate. Seriously! And spots! I saw shaky, vibrating pink spots on the walls. It's a strange experience. I wish I'd never tried it. I've done it quite a few times too many.

Laura, age 14

Dear Judy,
   My boyfriend, Jimmy, and I aren't getting along so hot lately. He got high with my cousin's best friend and starting kissing her (and more) in front of my cousin. When I found out I bawled my head off. Nothing mattered to me anymore. I had my entire life centered on that man. Sometimes I feel old and worn out and like I'm just another waste. I feel numb. Nothing could surprise me.
   Well, I'll look forward to hearing from you. Take care.

Love,
Laura, age 15

Dear Judy,
   Hey! I didn't break up with Jimmy after all. I love him too much. I never thought I'd feel like this. But I know now that it was my fault. I've decided to stop messing around with my life. You say I'm smart. If I can spend my spare time getting messed up out of my mind and *still make sense* I can imagine what it'd be like if I stayed straight. I could learn so much. My partying days are over, and I mean it. I mean it so much it hurts. And Jimmy is going straight too.
   I've decided that I want more out of life than hangovers and bad attitudes. I think that there's more of a purpose to life. It's just so, so, *so* hard.

This time will be the roughest I've been through and I hope, for my mind and sanity and *my* future children's lives, that I can do it. I hope so badly.

You see, it's not like it was those other times when I quit. Those other times I was having fun. I was getting high so easily and now it's over. I can't be tempted. I feel so low of myself to tell you this, it being the truth, but I have the habit now. I feel like pot has me in its grasp. I'm burned-out and in the fog and I hate it! I can't think straight sometimes. I can start off a sentence to someone and forget what I was talking about before I finish the sentence! It's crazy and unreal and there's no way to really describe it to someone who hasn't been there. It's like you're in a deep, dark hole in the ground, looking up, barely seeing grass and flowers at the top of the hole. Barely seeing the clear blue sky above you. Wanting to get out of that hole to feel the sunshine again. Smell the roses and run in the grass.

All I remember about being straight, which was a long time ago, is that I was real shy, got embarrassed *easy*, was confused about life and people and I preferred books to real life. They were my only refuge, my only escape.

Jimmy got busted last night for possession of marijuana. He's out now though. See, he was selling it. Pot. To keep up my *everyday* habit. And I *did* smoke everyday.

Anyway, I bawled my head off when I first heard about Jimmy getting busted. Later last night, after Jimmy got out, we had a talk. We talked about life and love and the way things are supposed to be. No busts. No getting stoned and forgetting about it. No copping out. Maybe I'm fooling myself *again* by trying to quit, but if you quit trying, you *know* it'll never work out. Usually when I'm trying to quit, and keeping my mind off pot, that's when people come over and spark it up. Right in my face. And I smell it before I have time to tell them I've quit, and the urge is there, always, and I give up to temptation.

It's like seeing a big, moist, scrumptious chocolate cake in your face and everyone else is eating it, loving it, but you're on a diet and can't have it. It's so hard to explain. It's much worse than chocolate cake when you're dieting, too. Lots worse. Pot grows to be a part of you. A part of your life. And changes hurt. They're so hard to make. A change in your entire life. In the way you think and look and act and feel. All for the better, but still so tough.

You've helped me get through some bad urges by being there to write to. If I hadn't written these letters I'd feel insane by now.

Love ya,
Laura, age 15

Dear Judy,
  Hey! Guess what?
  I haven't smoked pot in two days! Three counting today, but I can't count today until it's over. I'm taking this one day at a time. I swear, this is the longest I've been without it in a long, long, long time. But . . . no one's sparked one up around me in a while, though I have been offered liquor and turned it down. I'm just frantic that someone'll fire up a joint in front of me and I'll smell it. And want it so bad. I hear it takes thirty

days to get pot out of your system. I'm afraid I won't make it. I still get nervous when I think about it. Like I'm dying to taste it again. But I'm serious this time. I know I *need* to quit for good, to save my mind. I still feel like my mind's fogged up. Like I can't think or remember clearly. I have so much energy now, and I don't know what to do with it. I'm being driven up the wall.

Keep in touch.

Love,
Laura, age 15

Dear Judy,

Jimmy and I are doing all right. He quit selling heavily. The heat was on. Now it's only occasionally. Like when it's necessary.

You know what a lot of this is about? Low self-esteem. My dad treated me and my sisters and brothers—when we were kids—like we were shit. It stuck. If you're treated like shit, you feel like shit. I guess the feelings of low self-worth were passed on somehow, through genes or something.

Laura, age 15

Dear Judy,

With Jimmy and me it's like we're married. I love it, too. I can't wait till we really are married. I can't imagine life without him. I really can't. I've been with him since I'd just turned fourteen and now I'm almost sixteen.

I haven't the foggiest idea what I'm going to do after high school. I really don't. It upsets me, too. Yesterday I was so distressed about it I started bawling! I mean, I want my kids to be happy! I've been through so much bullshit in the short time I've been around. But, just like everyone else says, I'll probably end up working in the factory. When I'm old my hearing will be shot to hell, my back will be slumped over and my hands will be rough. Just like everyone else around here. I hate the idea of it!

But I plan to marry directly after graduation and have a family. It's what I've wanted (secretly) since I was fourteen. It's what I need. Security. Being with Jimmy is my security. I rarely ever feel secure or content or happy but on those rare occasions when I do, I've noticed I'm with Jimmy, cuddled up comfortably.

I thought about taking Marketing and Distributive Education I and II at the high school in eleventh and twelfth grades. They supposedly get you a job in that field (whatever it is!) during the time you take the courses, and after graduation, too. It's the only thing I know of to do after school that will insure me a job somewhere other than the factory. My algebra teacher wants me to go into computers, or think about it anyway, and she wants me to take four years of math, rather than the required three, because I'm good at it. I'm insecure about the thought of computers. I mean, they'd probably require college or something like that.

Do you have any ideas? Any would help.

Laura, age 16

279

Yes, I have ideas. I have urged Laura to see a counselor but she doesn't believe it would work for her. "You have to tell them the truth, don't you?" she has asked me. "Well, I could never tell a counselor the truth about my life."

Laura and Jimmy are still together. Last summer he took her to the beach for a vacation and her description of their time alone was filled with tenderness and love.

A month ago Laura wrote that she and Jimmy hadn't smoked any pot for six weeks. She was hopeful that it was "all over in that area." In the letter that followed, written two weeks later, she was depressed and sometimes feeling suicidal. After so much time in the fog she was afraid she might crack under the pressures of real life. Yet she realized that if she went back to smoking pot she might never try to quit again. I wish she had a support group to help her through this very difficult time.

When I write to Laura, I try to tell her how much her letters mean to me, how important *she* is to me. I worry about her. I feel relieved each time there is a letter telling me that she's okay. I encourage her to keep writing. I encourage her to stay in school and to think about ways of opening up her life. But only Laura can make those decisions. Even though there are adults, outside of her family, ready and willing to offer help, to offer Laura a chance, finally, it will be up to her.

Chapter XI
NOW THAT THEY'VE TOLD YOU . . .

Dear Judy,
Well, I'll bet you don't remember me. I'm Daphne. I wrote a couple of years ago and forgot to sign my last name and you had trouble reading my address because of my sloppy handwriting. Well, I got your letter anyway and I apologize for all that trouble. I've grown up through the years and you don't know what a comfort it is to read about kids your own age during these troublesome years of life. I'm still growing and making my way through society. I'm twelve now.

Daphne, age 12

I love the way Daphne writes about making her way through society. That's what growing up is all about and that's what the letters in this book have been about. It's impossible to grow up without problems. Kids have so little control over their own lives. They're

283

thrown into situations they didn't create and yet, they have to learn to cope. Control plays an important part in our relationship with our children. When they're small we have a lot of control over them. As they grow older we have to learn to give up that control and for some parents, that's hard. They have trouble letting go. Part of letting go is learning to trust. It shouldn't be so hard to trust our kids. After all, we raised them.

As I reread these pages I try to remind myself that there are at least two sides to every story. While I tend to identify strongly with kids, because they make a lot of sense to me, I am also a parent, and I know it's not possible to be all that our kids want us to be twenty-four hours a day.

Most kids genuinely love their parents and long for their approval. And they feel loved in return when their parents express a real sense of caring about them. They may fantasize about having our full attention whenever they want it, but they can accept the fact that we have other things going on in our lives (just as they do) as long as they know, deep inside, how important we think they are.

I've tried to give the kids a chance to say, in this book, what they wish they could say to you directly, what they wish you instinctively knew about them so that they would never even have to try to say it. Sometimes, when I'm talking with kids, I'll ask, "How are your parents supposed to know that?" and they will shrug and say, "Parents are supposed to know those things." But that's not necessarily true. Besides, parents don't always want to know. So I tell the kids, "It's up to you to help. You've got to try to tell them what's on your mind even though it's hard."

When Randy was growing up she would sometimes hand me a book and say, "Read this." By sharing books she was able to send me messages that she couldn't communicate in other ways. She was able to let me know *this is how I'm feeling . . . this is what I'm worried about . . . this is like us . . . this is the way I wish it could be between us.* Books can be bridges to communication between parents and kids, as can any shared experience. So, grab onto anything that helps you talk with your kids, anything that helps you exchange ideas. Eda LeShan, the psychologist, once told me that kids learn about life from us. The more we share with them, both facts and feelings, the better able they will be to cope. It's all right for them to see that we're not perfect, that we're only human.

"But children have changed so much," a woman I know told me recently. "My daughter is nothing like I was. Everything is so different today." Yes, some things are different. Family life has certainly changed. The rules have changed and there aren't a lot of new rules to replace them. But deep inside we're still far more alike than different.

Dear Judy,
I am a teacher in an alternative high school and I can tell you that kids haven't changed. What they most want to discuss are relationships and conflicts of value. The kids I know are most concerned about fights with their parents, making friends, sex, acne, music and death.

Wilma, adult

I don't think the letters in this book mean that kids today are more or less troubled than they were a generation ago. Their problems may be caused by different situations but their feelings about those problems and about themselves are the same.

Dear Judy,

I am a mother of three. People are always ranting about today's sophisticated teens. But in my opinion today's teens are similar in many ways to what we were. The same questions, guilts and insecurities seem to plague them.

Jeanne, mother

And the same questions, guilts and insecurities plague us, as parents. I'm sure my mother will wonder why I remember the events I wrote about in this book, just as I sometimes wonder why Randy and Larry choose to remember the very occasions I would most like them to forget. None of us wants to be reminded of our foolish mistakes, or of the hurtful behavior we've displayed toward those we love most.

When Randy and Larry talk about having their own children, we joke and laugh about what kind of grandmother I will be. They know that I will enjoy their children. They see me playing on the floor with them, teaching them to make "Junior Doo-dah Bird" faces and reading to them in different voices, the way I did with them. Yet they vow that they won't make the same mistakes in raising their children as John and I did with them. I know just how they feel. When I was a college student, majoring in early childhood education, I was so sure of it all. I would never repeat my parents' mistakes when I had children of my own. It seemed so simple then. Now I know it's not. The best advice I can offer, should my kids ask, is to rely on their own common sense and their senses of humor. I'm not sure anyone can ever be adequately prepared for parenthood. We learn as we go. We do our best and hope it will turn out okay.

I sometimes take out the family photo album and, like all parents, as I slowly turn the pages I wonder where the time has gone. Those adorable babies have grown up. They are in their twenties now, out of college and pursuing careers. They like to remind me how lucky I am to have them. As if I don't know! When I am concerned about what they are doing (Randy is a pilot and Larry will think nothing of dashing off to another country to work on a film) they ask me to imagine what it would be like if they had turned out to be boring. I laugh when they talk that way. Boring is not a word I would use to describe them.

I used to worry about losing touch with kids once my own were grown, but thanks to my young readers that doesn't seem likely. Their letters do more than keep me in touch. They soothe the sting of unfavorable reviews, make the censors look foolish and help me to keep writing, even when I feel I can't handle the loneliness of doing another book. Compiling this book has made me feel as if I have been through years of analysis. I haven't. But because of the kids who have written to me I've made some important discoveries about myself and my family. They have helped me to see more clearly and to be more forgiving, even of myself.

We can't solve our children's problems or protect them from reality. They live in the same world as we do. Their concerns are equally important, often they're the same. But we can try to prepare them for life, by talking with them and listening to them, not only to the spoken messages, but the unspoken ones as well. We can laugh with them, teaching them the value of humor, which often gets us through the tough times. We can be there for them, offering support and encouragement. We can help them learn to make wise decisions. We can give them the chance to change their minds and to learn from their own mistakes. We can try not to judge them for their opinions and their differences. Most of all, we can let them know how much we care.

Last summer I met a friend at a party, and as we were chatting he told me what it was like for him to become a father for the first time, at fifty. "You were smart," he said. "You had your kids early and got it out of the way."

I looked at him as if he were crazy. "You never get it out of the way," I said. "Once you're a parent it's forever!"

Resources

Because there are so many books available on the topics we have discussed, I cannot even attempt to provide a comprehensive list. I have suggested a few nonfiction books that I think are particularly helpful, but I have concentrated my efforts on giving the names of resource agencies and groups that may be able to help you or put you in touch with others who can. Many of these agencies offer selected reading lists.

You might also talk with the librarian at your public library, who could suggest just the right book or books for you and your family. Both nonfiction and fiction are important when you're dealing with these emotional topics—nonfiction to present the facts, fiction to identify feelings and help in understanding them. But no one book is right for every child or for every family.

If you contact any of these agencies, please keep in mind that addresses change (I haven't listed phone numbers for that reason but you can get them from directory information). Remember, many of these organizations are staffed by volunteers. Unless it's an emergency try not to get discouraged if you don't reach the right person easily.

Subjects are listed in alphabetical order.

Adoption

Your local adoption agency should offer programs, advice and reading suggestions on all matters relating to adoption.

*

> KREMENTZ, JILL. *How It Feels to Be Adopted*. New York: Alfred A. Knopf, 1982.

Nineteen boys and girls, from ages eight to sixteen, share their feelings about being adopted. The book is illustrated with photographs of the children and their families.

Alcoholism

> Al-Anon Family Group Headquarters, Inc.
> P.O. Box 182, Madison Square Station
> New York, NY 10159-0182

If you have a problem with alcohol, or someone close to you does, Al-Anon can give you information about support groups in your area. One of them, Alateen, helps the children of alcoholic parents. You can probably find Alcoholics Anonymous listed in the white pages of your phone book. Most communities also have other alcoholism treatment programs and family support groups.

*

> National Council on Alcoholism
> 12 West 21st Street
> New York, NY 10010

This is a public information agency that will refer you to local affiliates. They will also send information on request.

Child Abuse

Most cities have a toll-free hotline number to report cases of child abuse. Look in the white or yellow pages of your phone book under CHILD ABUSE or call the operator and ask for a local or national number to call. These hotlines are staffed by caring professionals who have experience in dealing with child abuse. They will contact someone in your area to help you deal with the situation.

*

Childhelp
P.O. Box 630
Hollywood, CA 90028

Childhelp provides literature on child abuse and how to deal with it, including information on preventive measures. A list of books is also available. But most important, it maintains a toll-free national hotline staffed by professionals that offers crisis intervention service as well as providing information. Call 800 information for an up-to-date number for Childhelp.

*

Parents Anonymous
7120 Franklin Avenue
Los Angeles, CA 90046

This is an international self-help organization for parents under stress. It can direct you to local chapters and support groups.

*

National Committee for Prevention of Child Abuse
332 South Michigan Avenue, Suite 1250
Chicago, IL 60604-4357

This organization offers free information and a resource booklet.

*

If you are a parent and feeling out of control, afraid that you might hurt your kids, call one of these three groups.

Death

The Good Grief Program
295 Longwood Avenue
Boston, MA 02115

This group offers a comprehensive bibliography of books and films on death and dying, prepared for children and adolescents. They also have a guide entitled *Helping Groups of Children When a Friend Dies,* designed for younger age groups.

*

LeShan, Eda. *Learning to Say Good-By: When a Parent Dies.* New York: Avon, 1978.

For children.

*

For adult readers I also recommend the books of Elizabeth Kübler-Ross, M.D., who has written extensively on the subject of death and dying.

Depression. See *Suicide and Depression*

Divorce

Rofes, Eric, ed. *The Kids' Book of Divorce.* New York: Random House, 1982.

This is the book that I send to kids who seem especially troubled by their parents' divorce. It's a good book for all kids who are going through the trauma of family separation. It's written by kids, for kids, and edited by their teacher at the Fayerweather Street School in Massachusetts.

*

Gardner, Richard. *The Boys and Girls Book About Divorce.* New York: Bantam Books, 1971.

Another straightforward book about kids and divorce.

*

Parents Without Partners
International Headquarters
7910 Woodmont Avenue
Bethesda, MD 20814

An organization dedicated to the welfare and interest of single parents and their children. They will provide free information and literature as well as a reading list for kids and parents. Local chapters have regular meetings and sponsor educational events. Look in your phone book to see if there is a chapter in your area, or contact international headquarters for further information.

*

Family Life Center, Inc.
Twin Rivers Road
Columbia, MD 21044

This is a local program of support services for children and their families who are experiencing divorce. They offer a brochure called *Talking to Children About Separation and Divorce* that is available on request.

*

Remember, there are many community programs available through schools or Y's, churches, synagogues and other organizations. I wish I had shared a program with my kids when we were going through divorce. It might have helped us talk about some important feelings.

See also *Stepfamilies*.

Drug Abuse

National Clearinghouse for Drug Abuse Information
5600 Fishers Lane
Room 10A-43
Rockville, MD 20857

The NCDAI provides a free bibliography and other information. It's always a good idea to get all the information you can before discussing a subject like drugs with your kids. You should also make this information available to them.

*

Nar-Anon
P.O. Box 2562
Palos Verdes Peninsula, CA 90275

This is a self-help program for people who are abusing drugs, or have family or friends who are. It is similar, in its methods, to Al-Anon. They also operate Nar-Anon Preteen (for children) and Narateen (for adolescents). For information about local chapters contact Nar-Anon at the above address.

There are local hotlines to call about drug problems. Sometimes these numbers are listed in the classified section of your local newspaper. You can also check in your phone book or call your Operator for information.

Family Violence. See *Alcoholism, Child Abuse, Incest and Rape*

Illnesses and Disabilities

The National Self-Help Clearinghouse
33 West 42nd Street
New York, NY 10036

There are over forty clearinghouses nationwide. You can get a list by writing to the above address. The clearinghouse in your area will then be able to direct you to organizations, support groups and other resources regarding your particular problem or interest.

The national clearinghouse can also provide the name of any national foundations dealing with the particular disabilities and illnesses of concern to you. These foundations offer bibliographies, information and newsletters. For example, I am familiar with the work of The Scoliosis Association, Inc., because the subject of my book *Deenie*. When kids write to me about scoliosis, I put them in touch with The Scoliosis Association.

One Penn Plaza
Department JB
New York, NY 10119

The Association is a membership organization of scoliosis patients, their families, interested professionals and other concerned people. It publishes a quarterly newsletter, *Backtalk,* that provides the latest information on scoliosis and its treatment.

Chapters of the Association have been formed throughout the United States, with affiliates in Europe and Canada. These chapters provide opportunities for scoliosis patients and their families to get together to learn more about the condition, its treatment, and how others have coped with it. Many chapters maintain youth groups and adult scoliosis patient groups, and carry on service projects benefiting hospitalized scoliosis patients. For persons living in areas where there is no local chapter, the national association can find a pen pal.

So, call The National Self-Help Clearinghouse (listed above) to find out if there is a similar group that can help meet your (or your children's) special needs.

See also *Learning Disabilities*.

Incest and Rape

Call the Rape and Sexual Abuse Crisis Center or the Women's Crisis Center nearest you. If you can't find either listed in the white or yellow pages of your phone book and it is an emergency, call your Operator or call one of the hotlines noted under Child Abuse.

See also *Child Abuse*.

Learning Disabilities

Foundation for Children With Learning Disabilities
99 Park Avenue
New York, NY 10016

This is a national voluntary organization dedicated to educating the public and increasing its awareness of such disabilities. They offer a book, *The F.C.L.D. Guide,* which defines learning disabilities and discusses how to discover and deal with them. It also lists national organizations, government agencies, learning-disabilities information centers and sources of material to help learning-disabled children and their parents. They publish *Their World,* an annual magazine with articles about and for those with learning disabilities.

Moving

NIDA, P. C., and W. M. HELLER. *The Teenager's Survival Guide to Moving.* New York: Atheneum, 1985.

Maybe it will help.

Parenting

There is so much available on the subject, I don't know where to begin. Parenting guides and how-to books can't hurt and some of them certainly could help, by offering insights and information. But remember, you don't have to follow the advice of every expert. If it feels wrong to you, don't do it. Rely on your own common sense first.

I once got advice from my pediatrician that felt all wrong to me. Yet I thought that because *he* said it *I* had to do it. It took me a long time to realize that there is good advice and bad advice. So look for a reasonable approach when you're choosing books on parenting, an approach that makes you feel comfortable.

＊

SPOCK, BENJAMIN, M.D., and MICHAEL ROTHENBERG, M.D. *Dr. Spock's Baby and Child Care* (40th Anniversary edition). New York: Pocket Books, 1985.

Still the best commonsense book about raising kids.

＊

CAINE, LYNN. *What Did I Do Wrong? Mothers, Children, Guilt.* New York: Arbor House, 1985.

This is a book for mothers, especially, since we tend to blame ourselves for everything that happens to our children.

Rape. See *Incest and Rape*

Reading

Twenty-three million adults in this country cannot read. You can help by calling 800 information and asking for the number of the CONTACT Literacy Center. They will give you information on literacy programs in your area. If someone you know cannot read, help them take advantage of these opportunities. If a parent can't read to his or her kids when they're small or share books with them when they're older, the family is missing an important way of communicating. You can also get more information or become a volunteer yourself by contacting either:

Literacy Volunteers of America
404 Oak Street
Syracuse, NY 13210

Or:

> Laubauch Literacy Action
> Box 131
> Syracuse, NY 13210

If you want information on reading programs for children contact:

> National Reading Is Fundamental
> 600 Maryland Avenue S.W., Suite 500
> Washington, DC 20560

Runaways

> National Runaway Switchboard

This is a national hotline designed to help children who have run away and their families. Call 800 information or your Operator for the toll-free number in your area.

Sexuality Education and Information

The organization to contact for sexuality information and education is Planned Parenthood. It offers so many services I can't begin to list them all here. Planned Parenthood will send bibliographies on request, on topics such as talking about sex with your children. It provides services for all ages, including information on pregnancy prevention, birth control, and abortion. Find out what programs your local affiliate offers. Check the white pages of your phone book or write or call:

> Director of Education
> Planned Parenthood Federation of America, Inc.
> 810 Seventh Avenue
> New York, NY 10019

If you're a teenager and you need information, you can call Planned Parenthood. If you are pregnant and don't know what to do, Planned Parenthood can explain your options and provide the information that will help you make the best decision. These services are confidential.

*

SIECUS (Sex Information and Education Council
of the US)
80 Fifth Avenue
New York, NY 10011

This agency maintains an information service and makes available reading lists and curricula for use in grades K–12. It welcomes phone and mail inquiries and will provide brochures and pamphlets on request. SIECUS can also refer you to other sources.

*

When it comes to sexuality education and information, I recommend the books of Sol Gordon, Mary Calderone and Eric Johnson. All three write books that are clear and to the point. If you go to the library or bookstore armed with only these names, you should do very well. A few of their titles are:

CALDERONE, MARY S., M.D., and ERIC W. JOHNSON. *The Family Book About Sexuality*. New York: Harper and Row, 1981.

This book is designed to answer the questions of every family member in direct, specific and understandable terms and to build a positive, responsible understanding of sexuality. It also includes a reading list and a concise encyclopedia and index for readers needing quick information.

*

CALDERONE, MARY S., M.D., and JAMES W. RAMEY, ED.D. *Talking With Your Child About Sex*. New York: Random House, 1983.

This book will help parents answer questions at each stage of the child's development, from infancy to puberty. It also contains a bibliography for children.

*

GORDON, SOL, and JUDITH GORDON. *Raising a Child Conservatively in a Sexually Permissive World*. New York: Simon and Schuster, 1983.

The Gordons tell parents how they can become "askable" and able to talk to their children comfortably about sex. It also provides an excellent bibliography and source list, not only regarding sexuality, but other family subjects as well. Sol Gordon has also written many books about sexuality for young readers.

*

JOHNSON, ERIC W. *Love and Sex in Plain Language* (Fourth edition). New York: Harper and Row, 1985.

A classic book for kids, it presents basic information on sexuality, emphasizing that it should always be seen in the context of the total personality and expressed in responsible, respectful, caring relationships.

*

RAJ Publications
P.O. Box 18599
Denver, CO 80218

This group publishes booklets that are short, to the point and very readable. Even kids who think they don't like to read will enjoy the presentation and gain a great deal of valuable information. I know of a library that purchased thousands of these booklets to leave around, hoping that teens would take them. They did. You may want to send for their list, then order just one or two booklets to be sure you feel comfortable with the presentation. Two of the titles available for your kids are:

The Perils of Puberty

For girls. It explores the physical changes and how to handle them.

The Problem with Puberty

The same, for boys.
I'm all for giving both booklets to boys and girls.

*

A few other books I really like:

ANDRY, ANDREW C., and STEVEN SCHEPP. *How Babies Are Made*. New York: Time-Life Books, 1968.

This is the book that helped me tell my children.

*

BELL, RUTH, et al. *Changing Bodies, Changing Lives*. New York: Random House, 1981.

I give this book to older teens (from about age fifteen). It discusses how to deal with the emotional, physical and psychological changes that occur during the teen years. What makes this book special is that in it, teens share their feelings and experiences in their own words. It also has helpful drawings and photographs. Ruth Bell wrote this book with the Boston Women's Health Book Collective, authors of *Our Bodies, Ourselves*.

Stepfamilies

Stepfamily Association of America
28 Allegheny Avenue, Suite 1307
Baltimore, MD 21204

Write or call to find out if there is a chapter in your area. If there is, go to their monthly meetings. They have support groups for each member of the stepfamily. Even if there isn't a chapter nearby, you can join the national association. They publish the *Stepfamily Bulletin*, featuring articles, book reviews and other information of value. The *Bulletin* is distributed free to members. This is *must* reading, not only for those who are already part of a stepfamily but for anyone contemplating marriage to someone who is a parent.

Suicide and Depression

> KLAGSBRUN, FRANCINE. *Too Young to Die: Youth and Suicide* (Fourth edition). New York: Pocket Books, 1984.

This is an outstanding book on the subject, for adults as well as teens. It provides a list of hotlines and suicide prevention centers around the country.

*

American Association of Suicidology
2459 South Ash Street
Denver, CO 80222

This is an information clearinghouse. It has an up-to-date nationwide listing of hotlines.

*

If you or someone you know is in need of help right away, ask your Operator to give you the number (or to connect you directly) with the nearest suicide or crisis intervention center in your area. Don't wait!

*

While the above agencies or books may not be able to solve your problems, it's well worth a few phone calls or letters to get the information you need to help you help yourself and your kids. Good luck.

In Praise of
Judy Blume
One of America's Most Respected Authors

"**SMART WOMEN** MAY JUST BE THE MOST EMOTIONALLY SATISFYING BIG BESTSELLER... TRIGGERS BOTH LAUGHTER AND TEARS...YOU'LL BE UTTERLY CAPTIVATED."–*Working Woman*

"**WIFEY** WORKS PERFECTLY!...WIT, PATHOS AND THE RING OF REAL LIFE!"–*Los Angeles Examiner*

"...**FOREVER**, A CONVINCING ACCOUNT OF FIRST LOVE."–*The New York Times Book Review*

"**LETTERS TO JUDY** IS A MOVING COLLECTIVE PORTRAIT OF YOUNG AMERICANS...THE SOUND OF REAL LIFE PRACTICALLY LEAPS OFF THE PAGES."–*Los Angeles Herald Examiner*

____**LETTERS TO JUDY** 62696/$4.50
____**SMART WOMEN** 50268/$3.95
____**WIFEY** 50189/$3.95
____**FOREVER** 53225/$3.50

POCKET
BOOKS

**Simon & Schuster Mail Order Dept. MWM
200 Old Tappan Rd., Old Tappan, N.J. 07675**

Please send me the books I have checked above. I am enclosing $_____(please add 75¢ to cover postage and handling for each order. N.Y.S. and N.Y.C. residents please add appropriate sales tax). Send check or money order—no cash or C.O.D.'s please. Allow up to six weeks for delivery. For purchases over $10.00 you may use VISA: card number, expiration date and customer signature must be included.

Name_____

Address _____

City _____ State/Zip _____

VISA Card No._____ Exp. Date_____

Signature _____ 549